LEADING BUSINESS
by the BOOK

LEADING BUSINESS
by the BOOK

Principles for a Fulfilling Business Life

Malcolm Evans

with

Jerry Pattengale

TRIANGLE PUBLISHING
Marion, Indiana

Leading Business by the Book
Malcolm Evans with Jerry Pattengale

Direct correspondence and permission requests to one of the following:

Triangle Publishing
Indiana Wesleyan University
1900 West 50th Street
Marion, Indiana 46953

Web site: www.trianglepublishing.com
E-mail: info@trianglepublishing.com

The *Chicago Manual of Style* is the preferred style guide of Triangle Publishing.

Published by Triangle Publishing
Marion, Indiana 46953

ISBN: 978-1-931283-36-6

All Scripture quotations, unless otherwise indicated, are taken from the *Holy Bible, New International Version*®. *NIV*®. Copyright © 1973, 1978, 1984 by International Bible Society. Used by permission of Zondervan. All rights reserved.

Scripture quotations marked (KJV) are taken from THE HOLY BIBLE, KING JAMES VERSION.

Used with permission of The Helen Steiner Rice Foundation, Cincinnati, Ohio. © 1965 The Helen Steiner Rice Foundation. All rights reserved for "A Bend in the Road." © 1972 The Helen Steiner Rice Foundation. All rights reserved for "Give Lavishly." "The Bridge Builder," by Will Allen Dromgoole, taken from: http://www.cordula.ws//poems/bridge.html, accessed 9/11/2008.

Cover design: Creative Fuel Design
Graphic design: Lyn Rayn

Printed in the United States of America

This book is dedicated to my wonderful wife, Nadine,
for enduring nearly forty years of conforming to changing time
schedules, preparing late meals, and running a taxi service for
our children while I pursued my chosen vocation.

Jerry would like to dedicate this work to
Ken and Cathy Rowe, who have demonstrated that a successful
business can help to build a strong family, and vice versa.

Contents

Foreword by Dave Dravecky   9

Acknowledgments   11

Introduction: The Concept of the Silent Partner as Senior Partner   13

1. Draw Maps with Clear Signs   17

2. Measure Well Your Steps and Missteps   31

3. Personal Loyalties Have Corporate Consequences   43

4. Doing or Delegating: Knowing When to Listen or to Let Go   55

5. Feed the Good Horses Well   67

6. Expect the Unexpected   79

7. Exercising Your Options Is a Healthy Workout   91

8. Wise Advice Is to Seek It   109

9. Givers and Takers   121

10. Plan Your Work then Work Your Plan   131

Appendix: Topical Advice from the Business World   141

Notes   145

About the Author and Contributors   151

Foreword

Over the years I have had the unique privilege of knowing Malcolm and his family. I have known him to be a man of deep conviction, integrity, and humility. Through his years of experience he has become a man of incredible wisdom. But more importantly, Malcolm has a great love for people, and an even greater love for God. As a result, of this he has written *Leading Business by the Book: Principles for a Fulfilling Business Life*. I believe his desire in writing this book is to take his passion and gift, being a successful business man, and to share his acquired wisdom, with us!

He has put careful thought into how this book can be a tool to help us. Whether you are a business professional, a business owner, or in the classroom with a dream to be a successful business person, Malcolm's desire is to help you do it by the Book! You will come face to face with ten principles that, have guided Malcolm in understanding how to lead business. As you may have guessed, the Book he refers to is God's Word. The Bible speaks of money and relationship just about as much if not more than anything else in Scripture. What better tool could be used in guiding us on this path?

Malcolm speaks of his Silent Partner in the introduction. That Silent Partner is God, "the One who has invested in him—giving him personal resources to succeed—and is there when he calls on him. Most importantly, His character traits transcend situations. His standards establish the fulcrum of business ethics. And, investments made with him pay eternal dividends." I like that! It puts doing business into proper perspective. The rewards are not temporal but eternal!

The other thing I like about Malcolm's approach is that God is not only his Silent Partner but his Senior Partner as well. That is so true whether in business or in life! Thank you Malcolm for guiding us to the One who gives meaning and purpose to all we do here on this earth. As you will see, this book contains so much more than just these two thoughts but I can't emphasize enough, it all begins as Malcolm says, with our Silent and Senior Partner.

As you read *Leading Business by the Book*, you will begin an adventure with Malcolm as he guides you with these time-honored principles in helping you to bring meaning and purpose to your business life. But I have a funny suspicion that you'll discover this book will help you do more than just managing your business well—it will also help you manage your life. And remember these principles are given not just to reap the benefits here on earth, but more importantly to reap the rewards eternally!

Malcolm, thank you for providing this valuable tool for such a critical time in our history!

Your Friend,
Dave Dravecky

Acknowledgments

Closing many deals during my decades in business was necessary preparation for writing this book. What I didn't realize, however, was the arduous journey from finishing the manuscript to realizing it in book form. Over three years after thinking I was finished, thanks to a host of people, you're holding this book in your hands.

I'd be remiss not to share my real introduction to the writing world. Although I had been to various authors' forums and workshops for novices, the reality was that being a successful businessman didn't make me a successful writer, no matter how many hours I invested—and they were many. Similar to my business ventures which we'll discuss later, I realized the need to surround myself with gifted people (in this case, in the writing world), and through this process was able to move forward.

The Tree of Life café in Marion, Indiana became a regular meeting place with a young friend who would eventually write this book with me. At a time when he had several books of his own under contract, it became a special challenge and goal to recruit him. After luring him with coffee several times to help me edit, "to give me feedback," he finally shared,

"Malcolm, I'm going to help you rewrite this one cup of coffee at a time if I don't agree to write this with you!" Part of successful business is being tenacious—but then he turned the tables and informed me of the long process ahead. I learned that the manuscript I thought was finished was but the first of many drafts. Early on, Jerry relayed the wisdom of the late Bob Briner, who shared with him (and also in *Roaring Lambs*) that we live in an age when Christians desire immediate gratification without the sacrifice needed for quality. And Bob's right. Though years ago I desperately wanted to share my principles with young business men and women, now I do so in a form with more staying power.

Dr. Harriet Rojas also contributed significantly by adding the reflection sections and the appendix, in addition to piloting this with business students at her university. She's been successful in launching ideas nationally, such as attested in the SIFE awards, and her assistance has helped to turn this into a book with applications for group dialogue.

Our publisher, Nathan Birky, believed in the project, and helped see it through. His business background provided an interest and empathy for bringing this to fruition. Likewise, Theresa Patterson and the extended editorial staff at Triangle Publishing were helpful all along the way. Mark Shanks and the *Creative Fuel Design* team helped with various versions of the cover and jacket design, and Alleta Tippey with many of the logistics.

Dave Dravecky continues to amaze me with his ministry, and in this case, with his assistance with the foreword during this busy season of his life. Thanks, Dave.

And I'd be remiss not to acknowledge my son, Jeff, for his role in prompting me to take up my pen. Sometimes it takes several nudges before we commit to something that adds value to our lives in a unique way, especially when it requires action outside of our comfort zone. More importantly, I trust that my son's deeply held conviction is true. That is, that the principles he applies in his own business life—the ones found in the following pages—will add value to your life as well.

—MALCOLM EVANS

Introduction

The Concept of the Silent Partner as Senior Partner

Some millionaires earned their money by giving advice to others, applying business schemes that solicit funds from business men and women. That's quite a feat—becoming wealthy by giving business advice while having no business experience. Others earned their millions sharing advice after initial business success. Tim Sanders is a good example of this category; he used his remarkable Yahoo! marketing plan to gain an international audience, and explains his approach in his best-selling book, *Love Is the Killer App*. This GQ fellow is worth a read even for us veterans. While young entrepreneurs like Tim have produced helpful management materials, and even some inexperienced business speakers offer helpful morsels, there is another group offering advice to the business world—and that's where I come in.

I am a white-haired investor. A retiree of sorts. I'm among the AARP veterans that get a bit sentimental when asked for advice. We're the ones that made it through our working lives and were dubbed "successful." Sometimes we got lucky, sometimes not. Over the long haul, however, some invaluable lessons surfaced. We may have lost millions along the way, but we made enough to compensate.

Over our careers, sound management principles rather than luck won the day.

Most importantly, my group of quasi-retired investors is thankful for the blessings we have received and realize that key principles guided us. In turn, we give back because it brings fulfillment. We give back because it flows from the philosophy that governed our business lives. My forty years in the business world have produced some wonderful adventures, a life of luxury according to some standards—and a life of giving. These same decades have accented the value of *Leading Business by the Book*.

The Book in question is the Bible. Plain teachings. Simple truths. Profound wisdom for both Christians and non-Christians. Its teachings proved instrumental in my journey to gain and sustain wealth. More importantly, my life has amounted to more than money. I've collected memories that I can live with and possessions I can die without. My life's purpose isn't simply about obtaining money, but obtaining money for a higher purpose.

"I've collected memories that I can live with and possessions I can die without. My life's purpose isn't simply about obtaining money, but obtaining money for a higher purpose."

This text utilizes some of my business stories, with glimpses of those of Jerry as well, leaving you with principles for financial and life success. In the end, the higher purpose of your life may not be spiritual like mine, but attaching income to a noble cause helps to sustain the passion for managing business and wealth.

When I drive by buildings carrying my name, or hear from individuals I've helped in business, I thank God for a guidebook that brought others joy through me. His Word not only kept me sane through both tough business deals and remarkable days, but also helped to form principles that led to financial freedom. Many of my greatest investments came from simple ideas mixed with sound decision-making and management practices, and followed by confident closure.

Choices come in different forms. Whether you own your own business or run another's company, or whether you manage a small operation, a division, or a large corporation, the principles of management are the same. Some decisions are routine in nature. We know exactly what to do and when to act. Some decisions are unprecedented. We have no past experience or case studies to consult. Other decisions allow considerable deliberation and a thorough response. And then there are the spontaneous decisions. No teammates to consult. No board members around. Nothing to go by but sensible principles from tested turf and, if you're wise, principles that are grounded in biblical truths. One of the keys you'll find in my business approach is that if you manage by the Book, your best resource never changes and is always at your fingertips.

These principles have been my personal guide for decades as a CEO, manager, and investor. These management principles were initially driven by my growing knowledge of the Bible in the context of years in management—and a good dose of common sense. They have helped me to become a leader. Without them I would have certainly failed. With them I became reasonably successful as one would measure success in this life.

Leading Business by the Book recommends a Silent Partner who has weathered various challenges with people. A silent partner can be a complicated dynamic in some business situations, but here it's rather straightforward. God is my Silent Partner; he has invested in me—giving me personal resources to succeed—and he is there when I call on him. Most importantly, his character traits transcend situations. His standards establish the fulcrum of business ethics. And investments made with him pay eternal dividends. This might appear altruistic or romantic, but business deals aren't just about working for your immediate personal gain. They are about making a contribution beyond your own lifetime.

I've also come to discover that my Silent Partner is also my Senior Partner. There is always a guiding direction, always a sense of rightness and ought-ness in decisions. Countless other business leaders have found help in the same biblical source that underpins the message of this book.[1]

Their advice has helped me along the way, and you'll find their works and adages referenced at the end of each chapter for your further studies.

The concept of God as a Silent Partner and Senior Partner is not only intriguing, but inspirational. It's central to monetary and management success. As you read this book you'll find practical ways to navigate your business days. You'll also find a personal code that will allow your retirement reflections, whether current or far into the future, to be ones weighted more by satisfaction than regret. I've missed my share of good deals, but in the end, it's not significant. I've made my share of killer deals, but in the end, they're not my greatest joy in life.

People often approach me for money. Life situations and noble causes often place people in tough situations. Others ask for my hand in starting a business. Perhaps some ask for ignoble reasons. But whatever the nature of the request, it's clear that borrowed money is a temporary solution at best. *Leading Business by the Book* brings long-term relief and lifetime success. It is my hope that you not only read the stories from my business journey in the Malcolm in the Marketplace sections, but apply the universal principles surrounding them.

I'm constantly aware that my investments have given me a voice with many audiences. For that I am thankful. It's an awesome privilege, and with an awesome privilege comes an awesome responsibility.

I'm joined in this writing enterprise by a young friend and national speaker, Jerry Pattengale. He's a writer and educator, and has worked closely with one of the nation's wealthiest families. He has also raised tens of millions of dollars for good causes, invented a few things, and this year alone has six books surfacing with various publishers. He also encouraged me to develop and rewrite my thoughts—a journey to make this text more helpful for the long haul. Together, we hope that you find this book a meaningful guide to a fulfilling life in the field of business.

MALCOLM EVANS
Marion, Indiana
August 2008

1

Draw Maps
with Clear Signs

I will instruct you and teach you in the way you should go;
I will counsel you and watch over you.

—Psalm 32:8

Directors without Direction Create Actors
with a Short Stage Life

Have you ever walked out of your boss's office not quite sure of your marching orders? Or, have you dreaded an upcoming meeting where you weren't sure of your own agenda items? It's frustrating to have hired— or to work with—a manager with no map, no well-calculated plan of action.

DILBERT: © Scott Adams/Dist. by United Feature Syndicate, Inc.

Avoid the Dilbert Dilemma

The scenario of a map-less manager reminds me of Scott Adam's *Dilbert* cartoon strip. It has attracted a national audience by poking fun at clueless managers.[1] Dilbert's pointy-haired boss usually gives directions that are obviously flawed, and audiences laugh out of empathy. Although the cartoon exaggerates for emphasis, managing is full of pitfalls. The greater the managerial position, the greater the potential for errors with serious impact. Evidence of this dynamic is portrayed in the NBC sitcom *The Office*, starring Steve Carell.[2] Whether he's inadvertently sending personal e-mails to his entire company or confiding in a loony employee who thinks he's a secret CIA operative, Carell constantly embarrasses himself. Although fifteen million viewers tune in weekly to laugh at his incompetence, our smiles help us to learn little about competent management.

"The greater the managerial position, the greater the potential for errors with serious impact."

Take a moment and look at Dilbert's boss. Does any face come to mind that you could place beneath the pointy hair? If so, what have you learned from observing that person? Now comes the more important question: Do you think any of your employees have legitimate reasons to pin your picture over the face of the pointy-haired boss?

In contrast, there is an unbridled confidence when employees look over their bosses' shoulders and see their worn notes with underlined directions. As our friend Keith Drury notes: "The person with the plan is the person with the power."[3] There's no sarcastic laughter or pointy-haired sketches when I've been around effective managers.

As an employee, have you ever stopped to think that the miles you were about to tread on a project that had been covered many times in your manager's mind, in his meetings, in his budget sessions, and in print? A manager spends countless hours behind the scene planning, envisioning possible outcomes, and troubleshooting before problems even arise.

Good managers realize that we're watching. They mentor in their unique ways, noticing the curious eyes and observation of their employees.

Most successful managers learn early to draw the map after reasoned input and before designating authority. They underline the route before outlining responsibilities. And, they show the marked map often.

Effective management has clear directions, and productive managers know where they're headed.[4] The flow charts aren't convoluted. Policies aren't mysterious. Procedures are not made on a whim, but through an established process. Information isn't held tightly or kept from subordinates. The team is all on the same page; partners and subordinates see the same map and understand its coordinates. Otherwise, subordinates become frustrated and detached from the project, and the manager becomes consumed with action steps assigned to others.

Oftentimes, the top manager or administrator needlessly alienates the people designated to carry out a project by giving them vague directions. Again, it's difficult not to think of *Dilbert* or *The Office* while discussing such poor management practices. Unfortunately, many employees can empathize with these fictional office workers because they share a similar experience.

The person atop the flow chart should never stifle the flow of ideas and productivity. Otherwise the phrase, "It gets lonely at the top," suddenly takes on new meaning—we're lonely through mismanagement and position, not through successful management and expectations. Recipes for sustained wealth and fulfillment call for good plans with obvious buy-in by our employees.[5]

Malcolm in the Marketplace

I can recall a memorable seminar with business professionals that occurred in 1991, and particularly an object lesson on the importance and effectiveness of clear planning. A few business colleagues traveled with me from Vienna, Austria, to find out if there was some way we could assist six former Communist countries on the mend. In addition to helping current businesses with their efficiency, we also hoped to assist those desiring to become business owners. Through three weeks of assessments, we saw predictable economic shortcomings, but were surprised that a common community request was assistance with business ethics.

After our initial tour, we regrouped back in the States and determined how best to respond to the list of needs. We formed a plan. Though our philanthropic group was not a panacea, it managed to assist in various ways. Among our most fulfilling efforts was a project that provided instruction in ethics, leadership, marketing, and public relations. In that context, we presented a lesson that applies to our current discussion.

A	B	C	D	E
1	6	11	16	21
2	7	12	17	22
3	8	13	18	23
4	9	14	19	24
5	10	15	20	25

Our plan was to capture their attention using available resources and to involve them in a learning exercise. In advance, the seminar leader randomly chose a column and number such as C-12, and secretly wrote the number on a piece of paper and laid it face down on the table.

The leader asked a random audience member to choose a column— A–E—from a white board. If the member chose A, the leader erased it. If C was chosen, all the columns but C were erased. Once C was the only column remaining, the leader proceeded with the rows, again asking members of the audience to select a row. If 12 was selected, all other rows were erased. Likewise, any number selected other than 12 was erased. The idea was to appear to offer free choice, but to force C-12 as that choice.

When C-12 was the only remaining option on the white board, the leader would reveal what he had written on the piece of paper that he had left on the table. Of course, it was C-12.

Rarely would anyone catch on to this little scheme until after the exercise was over. Some never caught on. The participant was led to the letter and number that had been chosen by the leader. The purpose of the exercise was then revealed: leadership must know where it is headed. We had set the stage to address their requested subject of business ethics—and then unfolded our plan.

The Reluctance to Set Definable Goals

One-year, five-year, and ten-year goals should be established and followed by any person or organization that wants to succeed. Your map (or route to success) needs clear signs to determine goal attainment or roads to failure. It seems silly to think some people don't have informed goals, yet many managers fail to use reasonable maps for success. Through the years, I've discovered two key reasons for this reluctance to set definable goals.

1. Measured failure

Do you know whether you are succeeding or failing in your management life? What test do you apply to determine the answer? We ask this because some managers do not want to know if they are failing. Success and failure can become visible when placed beside a goal chart. On a much lighter note, many wives joke that this same principle seems to apply to men following actual roadmaps. Men don't like to stop and ask for directions. They allegedly waste time hunting for the destination—and refuse to admit defeat. Unfortunately, there's likely some truth in this stereotype and in many business situations, regardless of gender.

2. Measured merit

How long has it been since you've stepped back to look at the big picture? You know—the one that shows where you're headed. Goals reveal a manager's vision, and its worthiness becomes not only public, but the source of much energy and expense. A vision becomes a double-edged sword. It's necessary to keep the team on target internally, but it also reveals the target externally. If the destination loses its luster the closer you get, or loses its value, it's a vision problem. That is, the goals lack merit overall. Without a vision, a business will flounder and eventually perish. Without a roadmap, you'll have no idea if you're on target.

Use a Map and Mark It

Whether it's a forty-page business plan, a wall graph, or a diagrammed Web site, all employees should know the plan. And whether it's felt marker notes or quotes on the web, they need to see your input.

The key to establishing a map is in knowing which questions you need to answer. While there are many categories of questions, marketing analysis is paramount in our planning. What products are wanted by a consuming public? What niche is there in the marketplace for our products or services (what makes our product the better choice)? Is some other company capable of producing our products or services for less money? What must we do to remain competitive?

Answers to these questions lead to the logistical questions: What are the sales forecasts, projected expenses and income, and what is our marketing plan? A major part of life success isn't knowing how to answer all questions, but how to choose those important ones worthy of your best energies. The same is true in business.

After reflecting on this chapter, write the following map dynamics on a card and place them by your computer monitor as a checklist for planning:

1. What questions do I need answered before making my next map?

2. What information do I already have to help answer these questions?

3. Where can I get additional needed information?

4. Which employees proved especially helpful with the last map?

5. Have other employees surfaced that can factor more prominently in the next master plan?

The 70/30 Dynamic of Your Role in the Plan

While numerous schemes exist for "minute management," I suggest that you schedule only 70 percent of your time on any given day. The remaining 30 percent is set aside anticipating unscheduled questions, requests, and necessary actions. Flexibility and margin allow for reflection and longer attention to promising developments. This 70/30 rule also helps to prevent decision making when you're exhausted. If some unexpected events have interrupted your day, then delay making important decisions until a later time.

The endemic problem of running schedules to the brink finds responses in *How Full Is Your Bucket?* by Tom Raft and Donald Clifton, as well as Richard Swenson's *Margin: Restoring Emotional, Physical, Financial, and Time Reserves to Overloaded Lives*. While Clifton and Rath emphasize the need for affirmation and recognition in the workplace, and note its absence as the leading reason for leaving jobs, Swenson highlights a way of taking control of out-of-control schedules. "People are tired and frazzled. People are anxious and depressed. People don't have time to heal anymore. There is a psychic instability in our day that prevents peace from implanting itself very firmly in the human spirit."[6] In the latter half of his book, he unpacks this formula around the subtitle: *Restoring Emotional, Physical, Financial, and Time Reserves to Overloaded Lives*. Through gaining a clearer understanding of *power* and *load* we are better situated to retain our vitality:

Power is made up of such factors as energy, skills, time, training, emotional and physical strength, faith, finances, and social supports.

Load is made up of such factors as work, problems, obligations and commitments, expectations (internal and external), debt, deadlines, and interpersonal conflicts.

When our load is greater than our power, we enter into negative margin status, that is, we are overloaded.

When our power is greater than our load, however, we have margin.[7]

Indiana Wesleyan University, which has around nine hundred employees (two hundred non-academic), recently had all its personnel read and discuss Swenson's book. The school also enforced vacation time for everyone. It's little wonder that *The Best Christian Workplace Institute* ranked the school among the top forty workplaces in the U.S. in 2007.[8]

While the above books afford many warnings and helpful suggestions regarding scheduling, the 70/30 rule is a great place to begin. Whether you are a top-level manager, a person who operates your own business, or someone in between, you must have flexibility in your plans for each day, week, month, and year. Plans for the distant future will likely change as new information arrives. And crises or opportunities can adjust daily plans. Your completed daily schedule will often vary from your intended agenda—but were the priority tasks addressed? The answer to that question is far more important than minute adherence to a schedule.

The Quadruple D Rule

A healthy practice to follow with items that cross your desk is the four Ds: do, delay, delegate, and don't. This is a helpful approach to plan your work and work your plan that will be discussed in chapter ten.

Do

Place into a pile on your desk those things which have come your way that you plan to do that day. You should develop your own formula on how to walk through these decisions—but whatever the formula, it needs to be quick.

Delay

Place into a pile on your desk those things which you plan to do at a later time. Again, have a formula in mind.

Delegate

Begin another pile which contains those things that have crossed your desk which you plan to give to someone else to do. Like your own "Do" decisions, also allow your employees the freedom to establish patterns without judging them on one or two examples. Feedback, however, is always appropriate.

Don't

Do not get involved in making decisions on items that do not involve you, even though others may be expecting you to do so. In this manner, guard your time and put the appropriate items into this pile.

"Excellent oversight of a faulty business plan will only minimize losses instead of maximizing gains."

A Good Business Plan Is a Prerequisite for Effective Management, and a Good Manager Is a Prerequisite for a Good Business Plan

Excellent oversight of a faulty business plan will only minimize losses instead of maximizing gains. The business plan helps to establish the basis for your budget. Small business owners are often left to develop business plans alone. If this is your predicament, obtain the services of a financial counselor or a business friend with sustained business success.

Business plans vary and include a sundry of variables. The ultimate question is whether a company can deliver a product or service for a profit. Secondary questions are those that help to form such an answer. They will include such things as:

- Do we own or lease the building where we have our operations?
- Do we own or lease the equipment that is needed?
- Where is our best location?
- Will we utilize rail or truck services?
- What personnel are needed?
- Will we acquire capital by borrowing from lending institutions or will we have investors?
- What type of corporation best suits our needs?
- What marketing techniques will be best suited for our business?

Consulting Your Silent and Senior Partner

Plan to pray for your business plan. There's a lot of truth to the modern proverb, "The best-laid plans of both mice and men do often go astray."[9] After all, we're only human. In addition to constant review of your plan to adjust to changing factors, have a constant prayer plan.

If you are in a position in your organization to gather together your colleagues on a weekly basis for prayer—do so. I did this with my entire home office staff over a period of ten years. During that time there was an absence of serious problems and financial catastrophes.

Psalm 32:8 says that if you want to know what the Lord wants you to do, simply ask him and he will guide you. Another key Scripture I began following early in my business years was Matthew 6:33: "Seek first his kingdom and his righteousness, and all these things will be given to you as well."

The best business partner you will ever have is the Lord Jesus Christ. He will give you wisdom beyond your years—wisdom that you do not currently possess. He can give you a peace when things are going well, and he can also give you a feeling of being peace-less when you need help and direction.

When one manages by the Book, income is more likely to increase, expenses will come under control, and your Senior Partner will care for you and your management efforts in unusual ways. I am not endorsing the so-called "health and wealth" prosperity gospel promoted by some televangelists. This tends to minimize and often ignore the realities of our humanness and of life's struggles.[10] Rather, I believe that God will help us with our work plan, and will bless us over the long haul for our obedience in seeking him in establishing sound business practices. He also helps us to learn from our mistakes.

Modern society has bought into a positive-thinking philosophy that often overlooks hardships. If it's not one's calling to be in business, why should that person expect the outcomes of those called into this line of work, especially if the others have a higher passion and preparation for it? Why should we equate the fulfilled life with financial gain, regardless of one's gifts and life calling? It's about as counterintuitive as me expecting success in music or teaching elementary school just because I'm a Christian. I believe that God blesses all of us in unique ways. To expect wealth simply because we're Christians is not consistent with the Word of God, which is replete with warnings about materialism. Neither does this expectation reflect the example of millions of Christians who have gone before us. A successful and fulfilling business life often does not coincide with gaining wealth or riches, but in reaching a positive income over investment—a lasting social or spiritual benefit—worthy of our best energies.

Questions for Reflection

As you begin this time of reflection, I ask you a primary question: If you don't have time to do a task correctly, when will you have time to do it over? Perhaps one of the lead questions below will prompt you to enhance an area of your managerial planning. Or, perhaps some of the sub-questions will be of assistance. I don't expect you to spend a lot of time with each of these questions, but to find a couple key ones that resonate with you and your present management situation.

1. Where are you headed as it relates to managing? Be totally candid—what is your key goal in management?

2. What is your game plan to reach your goals? What are the destination points on your map? If I walked into your main office, what would I see that provides evidence of your successes? Awards? Pictures of business ventures? Charts? Personal plaques? What would be seen that shows the direction for your business? If you were asked for a document of your personal management plans, what would you show?

3. How do you plan to keep your focus? How are you keeping the rest of life in perspective while pursuing business goals?

4. What counsel are you expecting from your Senior Partner? How often are you relying on the Word—the guide your Silent Partner has already given you to assist in your business journey?

5. Can you list three peers you meet with regularly? What is intentional about your time together? If you've been meeting with peers, are these beneficial times together? How are you determining their value?

6. Are you familiar with any of the resources that follow? If so, in
   what ways do they help? How would a systematic approach to
   such works be helpful? What about online helps? What Web
   helps have you found beneficial?

Additional Resources

Batson, Ted and Blake Neff. *Business Ethics: Sunday Ethics—Monday World* (Marion, Ind.: Triangle Publishing, 2007).

Brown, David. *Choices: Ethics and the Christian* (Oxford: Blackwell, 1983).

Chewning, Richard. *Business Ethics in a Changing Culture* (Reston, Va.: Reston, 1984).

Coles, R. *Lives of Moral Leadership* (New York: Random House, 2000).

Galloway, Dale. *On Purpose Leadership: Multiplying Your Ministry by Becoming a Leader of Leaders* (Kansas City, Mo.: Beacon Hill Press, 2001).

Hill, Alexander. *Just Business: Christian Ethics for the Marketplace* (Downers Grove, Ill.: IVP Academic, 1997).

Jones, David Clyde. *Biblical Christian Ethics* (Grand Rapids: Baker, 1994).

Lawrence, William. *Beyond the Bottom Line: Where Faith and Business Meet* (Chicago: Praxis Books, 1995).

Maxwell, John C. *The 17 Indisputable Laws of Teamwork: Embrace Them and Empower Your Team* (Nashville: Thomas Nelson, 2001).

Peace, R., L. Coleman, A. Sloan, C. Tardif. *Setting My Moral Compass* (Littleton, Colo.: Serendipity House, 1984).

Smith, Mark and Larry Lindsay. *Leading Change in Your World* (Marion, Ind.: Triangle Publishing, 2001).

2

Measure Well Your Steps and Missteps

But seek first his kingdom and his righteousness, and all these things will be given to you as well.

−Matthew 6:33

Small Actions Determine Large Outcomes

Entrepreneurs on the Forbes 400 list don't fool the tax assessors.[1] Their financial success is real, minimally 1.3 billion dollars each—at least for a season. They are examples of prosperity as defined by income levels. Likewise, communities tend to know if local business leaders are successful, but usually this is determined by whether they've sustained their success. The community sees their ability to buy and sell, and evaluates their consistency in character. People also judge business leaders on their dedication to putting the company and other managers over their own ambitions—a key trait of "Level Five Leadership" that Jim Collins highlights in his book *Good to Great*.[2] Collins discovered Level Five Leadership among the top eleven companies out of 1,400 that had been listed among Fortune 500 companies between 1965 and 1996. These eleven out-performed the market three to one during a fifteen-year period. Their executives were unique from the other companies; though they were equally as ambitious, they poured it into their companies instead of themselves.

"True character will stand the test of time— an investment with lasting dividends." They built enduring greatness through a paradoxical blend of personal humility and professional will. They were modest, often self-effacing, and always relied on inspiring standards (as opposed to inspiring charisma) to motivate employees. While business deals always involve resources, the difficult part is sustaining respect.

Perhaps the most remarkable accomplishment is to enjoy sustained respect from those within your organization. To lead by example involves not only the ability to make money, but to do so honestly. True character will stand the test of time—an investment with lasting dividends.

Malcolm in the Marketplace

A prerequisite for my managerial success was a personal growth plan, and I supported a wide array of growth plans for others as well. Attending workshops with successful people, regardless of their tie to the business world, proved fruitful. Oftentimes, I found motivations and transferable illustrations from the most unlikely sources.

Art Linkletter (b. 1912) is a prime example. He drove home an integrity lesson while speaking in Marion, Indiana, in 1985. While hosting, he shared a hilarious story from his volumes of interviews with children (his celebrated TV and book series, *Kids Say the Darndest Things*).

He asked a young boy, "What does your father do?"

"Oh, he's a cop," the boy replied.

"Well, that's a mighty dangerous job," Mr. Linkletter said.

"Yeah, he grabs criminals, searches them, and then takes them down to the slammer."

Art Linkletter replied, "I bet your mother fears for his safety at times."

The little guy answered, "Nah, she doesn't mind, 'cause Dad brings home lots of watches and rings and jewelry and stuff."

The moral is straightforward: never compromise your integrity because of circumstances. This reflects a major biblical theme. "In everything, do to others what you would have them do to you, for this sums up the Law and the Prophets" (Matt. 7:12).

I could share the illustration with my staff in a nonthreatening way during our group meetings. Like the advice in Tim Sander's *Love Is the Killer App,* developing and facilitating an environment of sharing new knowledge has many benefits for both the giver and the rest who receive. It also implies that there is an intentional effort to learn—to read, attend workshops, listen to Webinars, and to engage a host of new resources.[3] I'm nearly eighty and still frequent seminars.

Don't Substitute Gold for the Golden Rule

Whatever city or country you do business in, you'll find a parallel of the Golden Rule—often known as "the ethic of reciprocity." However, you'll discover that many of these are phrased in the negative sense. When Jesus presented the Golden Rule, he presented it in a positive fashion. You see, it's one thing to say, "Don't do to others what you don't want done to you." But it's quite another to follow Christ's words, "Do to others as you would have them do to you" (Luke 6:31).

Confucius said, "Do not do to others what you do not want them to do to you" (*Analects* 15:23). The Hindus teach, "This is the sum of duty: do not do to others what would cause pain if done to you" (*Mahabharata* 5:1517). Other religions seem to reflect Christ's positive view in concept but not in practice. For example, Islam teaches: "None of you [truly] believes until he wishes for his brother what he wishes for himself" (Number 13 of Imam Al-Nawawi's Forty Hadiths).[4]

Kindness Should Be Accompanied by Wisdom

How should we apply the Golden Rule in today's business world? This can be tough at times in today's marketplace. Jerry once developed the first pictorial directory software, only to have it stolen by a major company—even after disclosure agreements had been signed. Later he coined the word *enronic* after the greed of the Enron executives, and in the light of his firsthand view of unethical behavior.[5]

Jerry used to work for Robert Van Kampen. He asked the billionaire about his key guiding principles for success. The answer came in his usual blunt manner. "I treat every business partner as a snake—because we're all fallen creatures." That was a little difficult to stomach, and Jerry pressed him. "But as Christians, we're to practice the Golden Rule. How does this correlate?" Bob responded, "There's a difference between being kind and being smart. The two are not in tension."

We have a long line of Christian business men and women to look to for advice. One example is the work of the late Bob Briner, author of *Roaring Lambs*. This book calls for Christians to make a difference outside of the Christian subculture, and is replete with examples of those who have. Briner's work has launched various Roaring Lamb societies and those like The Society of World Changers at Indiana Wesleyan University. Though he was the winner of an Emmy Award with Arthur Ashe for "A Hard Road to Glory," the founder of the Association of Tennis Professionals (ATP) and ProServe Television, and was successful in many other business arenas, he consistently remained humble and promoted biblical principles in managing business and leading others."[6]

Millennials Are Dominating the Workplace and They Thrive on Intangibles

Our businesses are now employing a wave of millennial employees (those born after 1981).[7] According to the leading research, this group—likely including most of this book's readers—has seven key characteristics. They are:

1. Special

2. Sheltered

3. Confident

4. Team-Oriented

5. Achieving

6. Pressured

7. Conventional

While each of these characteristics has a significant influence on how we manage, the work of Tim Sanders helps to summarize three key principles that reflect the essence of the Golden Rule.

As previously mentioned, Tim is the guru behind much of the marketing success of Yahoo! During a presentation to a group of two thousand business executives and their community collaborators in Marion, Indiana, he spoke about intangibles in the workplace.[8] By intangibles Sanders is referring to unseen resources, specifically: knowledge, network, and compassion. Sanders expands on this in his fascinating book, *Love Is the Killer App: How to Win Business and Influence Friends*. His book outlines the philosophy that helped to establish his business reputation. And people are listening.

Sanders cautions, however, that it takes all three of the intangibles—knowledge, network, and compassion—to succeed with this new work force.

It's not enough to be smart and collaborative. The dynamics of intangibles radically affect one's work environment and extended business community.

Sanders calls people in the bizmarket who embrace his philosophy *lovecats* (a play on the third intangible, compassion).

He concludes that the third of his intangibles, compassion, is the most difficult for company executives to endorse. He argues:

> So what if some people laughed? So what if some people thought I was sucking up? Or sucking down? Or sucking sideways? The knowledge and the network—these are value-added and easy. Share the books, share the Palm Pilot: you can be fairly sure that these will be well-received and credible gifts. But consider sharing compassion! Consider overcoming the cold and impersonal behavior between clock-in and clock-out hours, consider conquering the urge to be noncommittal when it comes to feelings!
>
> Most people don't feel comfortable with workplace intimacy. But I say you've got to express your compassion, because, combined with knowledge and network, it is the way to win hearts and influence business in this, the dawn of the new business world.[9]

Tim Sanders climbed the success ladder in the business culture of the 1960s–70s. The rungs today are noticeably different—the ladder is now horizontal.

What would your business environment look like with these intangibles in place?

- A business community that systematically and spontaneously gains and shares knowledge.
- A business community that systematically and spontaneously shares contacts and encourages collaboration.
- A business community that systematically and spontaneously affirms positive characteristics and actions.

- A unique business community that systematically and spontaneously highlights the intangibles of knowledge, networking, and compassion to potential investors.

The reasons for embracing these intangibles are many, but a few seem to surface:

1. Intangibles assist business productivity.
2. Intangibles assisting productivity will, in turn, help retention of business.
3. Intangibles could be the deciding factor in establishing new business relations.
4. Intangibles could convince an entrepreneur to continue dialogue, even when other factors are in favor of a competitor.
5. These intangibles would resonate with the values of many community institutions (such as service organizations, religious groups, schools and colleges, as well as parent and neighborhood groups).

The beauty of the Sanders' model is that these new millennial workers have control over their most valuable resources and these resources are transportable. One's knowledge, network, and compassion are personal—not corporate—currency. They reflect the Golden Rule as well as the millennial preference. Therefore, if you're a CEO or the owner of a business, it's to your advantage personally and professionally to understand this generation's view of transferable resources—the intangibles.

If you're climbing up the ladder of success, pause and look around. In the new economy, you should be looking across horizontal rungs. After all, we're all human. And, that's the point.

Active Approaches

We need to be active, not passive, in our practice of the Golden Rule. Our world is suffering enough with people who just want to get by. Our challenge to you as a manager is to take the Golden Rule, as Jesus taught in the book of Matthew, and apply it to your business life on a daily basis. Set your course to live by principle, not just by rules.

Managers of business should practice a high standard of ethics in the work place. Some practical suggestions are as follows:

1. Give more than simply a fair day's work. Demonstrate your commitment by being at work before starting time as well as after quitting time.

2. Be trustworthy in every situation. Honesty and hard work will gain the appreciation of supervisory personnel.

3. Dishonesty will cause your best subordinates to desert you.

4. Don't bend the rules for personal gain. Wrong deeds will eventually create havoc in your life. We reap what we sow.

5. Be genuinely interested in others. This will cost you something— your time, your efforts, and sometimes your finances—but you will receive much more than you give.

Most people know, in theory, what is right. What secular ethics does not, and cannot provide, is the motivation for right action. Only the principles that are contained in the Golden Rule provide both the ethical standards and adequate motivation for right action. Practice the Golden Rule as Jesus taught: "Do to others what you would have them do to you."

I can look back across the years of my life and tell you that almost every business opportunity that has come to me when I was in a servant's role. Business contacts came when I was serving somewhere in a voluntary way, either on a board, or in some other capacity, giving of my time and talents for others. I did not plan it that way, but these were welcome, unintended consequences.

Businesses need well-trained, highly qualified, and dedicated Christian businessmen and women—people who are committed to a Higher Power and who refuse to compromise their integrity for anything or anyone.

Many opportunities come to business people. Some of them are good and some are bad. Many times temptations come along with these opportunities. The temptations come in a variety of ways, but they all lead to the same question: "Will it be my way, or God's way?" Oh, the temptation may not always be quite that obvious. It might be along the lines of: "Should I shortcut here and there in order to get ahead?" Following God's principles will require daily decisions to put him first.

Resolve to Have No Regrets

I mentioned previously about an opportunity that came my way to purchase or lease facilities at a time when our company really needed those acquisitions. Let me expound on this opportunity, showing how "resolve to have no regrets" actually played out in one key episode of my business life. It was during that same time that a man called me who was scheduled to gain several thousand dollars from one of the transactions. The problem was that this man was in the process of declaring bankruptcy and wanted me to help him shield those dollars from the bankruptcy court. Now the court had been notified as to the amount we were willing to pay for the facility. The caller was asking me to advise the court that he would be receiving several thousand dollars less than the agreed upon figure. He proposed that we get together at a much later date and split up the money. I hung up the phone and immediately called my attorney to advise him of my previous call. Needless to say, we proceeded to handle the transaction through the bankruptcy court in a proper and legal manner. Could I have made several thousand dollars doing it the illegal way? Yes, and I would have gained short-term benefits, but my business would have suffered for it in later years.

The measure of a person is what he or she does when alone. "The integrity of the upright guides them" (Prov. 11:3).

If we choose to follow the principles as taught in the Holy Word, then God takes the responsibility for the success or failure of the venture. If we choose to ignore him, then we may very well be headed for disaster. If, when we follow his ways, we end up with less, then it wasn't ours in the first place. It never pays to take what you have not been given.

The rewards of business will come to those who put God first in everything they do. Bankers will like to do business with you. Perhaps you will be able to find investment money or stockholders when others are finding it very difficult.

Employees will gravitate to employers who practice a high code of ethics. Their standard of performance will be elevated when they know what your standard is. Employees enjoy working for people who keep their word and who treat them fairly. Companies are now rated in national surveys on such things. The most valuable resource that any business organization has is its people—and they simply want to be treated with dignity.

When King Solomon's son, Rehoboam, came to the throne, he asked the elder statesmen of the nation how he should lead the people. Their answer: "If today you will be a servant to these people and serve them and give them a favorable answer, they will always be your servants" (1 Kings 12:7). But King Rehoboam ignored their advice and used his power and authority to manipulate, control, and exploit the people. As a result, the nation rebelled and he lost the kingship.

When we serve, we must always think first of the One we are trying to serve. Putting God first in your life and your business carries its own reward, although it does require self-discipline. Remember, as you determine to manage by the Book, that you will be tempted to traffic in the grey areas between right and wrong. The temptation will be to go ahead and do something because it is common practice. When we follow God's principles there are no grey areas to contend with and we focus on what God is doing, not on what those around us are doing.

Questions for Reflection

1. How do you treat your business associates?

2. Provide three examples that demonstrate your practice of the Golden Rule in working with business associates.

3. In what ways are you a servant when it comes to managing?

4. How do you measure success?

5. Give an example of a management decision you made which could have been handled better using a servant approach to leadership.

Additional Resources

Bloesch, Donald. *Freedom for Obedience: Evangelical Ethics in Contemporary Times* (San Francisco: Harper and Row, 1987).

Bonheeffer, Deitrich. *The Cost of Discipleship* (New York: MacMillian, 1975).

Collins, J. C. and J. I. Porras. *Build to Last* (New York: Harper-Collins, 1994).

Jones, Laurie Beth. *Jesus CEO: Using Ancient Wisdom for Visionary Leadership* (New York: Hyperion, 1995).

Kidder, R. *How Good People Make Tough Choices* (New York: Willima Morrow and Company, 1995).

McQuilkin, Robertson. *Biblical Ethics: An Introduction* (Wheaton, Ill.: Tyndale House, 1989).

Nash, R. H. *World-Views in Conflict* (Grand Rapids: Zondervan, 1992).

Rae, S. B. and K. L. Wong. *Beyond Integrity: A Judeo-Christian Approach to Business Ethics* (Grand Rapids: Zondervan, 1996).

Smedes, Lewis. *Choices: Making Right Decisions in a Complex World* (San Francisco: Harper and Row, 1991).

Williams, Oliver and John Houck. *Full Value: Cases in Christian Business Ethics* (San Francisco: Harper and Row, 1978).

3

Personal Loyalties
Have Corporate Consequences

And I will ask the Father, and he will give you another Counselor
to be with you forever—the Spirit of truth.

–John 14:16–17

The Tandem Qualities of Commitment and Dedication

Successful business men and women are aware of their own limitations as well as the limits of behavior. They are committed to the standards of the industry and their parameters. Oftentimes this involves ethical standards, but commitment also ties directly to standards of quality and efficiency.

While commitment involves loyalty to one's field of expertise, dedication in this sense involves loyalty to one's corporation. Whether you're in an entry level job where changing companies every two years is expected, or whether you're in a career position and are unhappy, dedication is essential. A very helpful adage that applies in transitional times is "Wherever you are, be there until you leave." And this applies even if it's five years until that departure finally comes.

Commitment and dedication work in tandem. We need always to keep in mind that our personal skill sets are transferable, and that we hone them through our dedication to a company—regardless of how healthy and wealthy it is, and these two are often not synonymous.

Malcolm in the Marketplace

The issue of employment perks can place any of us in tempting situations. While we can enjoy some wonderful benefits, I learned early on that some of these run contrary to my commitment to the standards of accounting, my field of expertise.

My refusal to take illegal perks put me at odds with one of my new bosses shortly after a decision to join his company. The tandem qualities created serious tension at the time, but later proved to be the transition from well-paid employee to partner in the business.

I had been rising through the ranks of a transportation corporation and was assured of a healthy and predictable salary for the rest of my career. However, I was looking for a change; I wanted to explore new possibilities. My worth to companies was due in large part to my accounting skills and decisions, and to the fact that they were transferable. So, I uprooted my young family and walked away from security. If it wasn't for the peace I had through prayer and the definite sense of peace about my new job in the health care industry, I would never have left for another state.

Looking back, the move proved to be a good one overall, but with it came some real testing. I discovered firsthand that not all business owners share my values.

During my first weeks on the job, my new employer encouraged me to buy my family's groceries on a company account, like he and his family had done for years. I declined the offer. In addition, I refused to let my family shop at places such as textile firms that provided linens for the facilities that we managed. I could have gone there on the company dime, but it was clear that it violated the standards of accounting I endorsed. The tension was that I was the new accountant for this growing chain of private nursing homes, the shining star that they expected to take them to the next level, but I was being encouraged to compromise my business and ethical principles. I also distinctly remember the day one of my bosses asked me to issue a check for "business receipts" when they were really expenditures for personal items. I refused to do this as well.

While this might seem like a black-and-white issue, emotions and obligations test you in new ways. But dear friends, keep in mind that these tests don't complicate matters. God has a divine plan and we'll never regret following what we know aligns with it. I had determined to follow God's acceptable accounting principles. Regardless of where you're working, you need to be committed to the standards of your field, but foremost be committed to God's excellent standards for you within that field.

I also was resigned to the dedication principle—to give the new position and company my best efforts. Although it's an arbitrary number, when these tensions developed I wanted to see it through for two years to fulfill my dedication to an employer and company. The period from my start date until the company owner passed away just fourteen months later were among the most intense I have weathered even until the present. I have a full head of white hair and I'm sure these months prompted the change.

Halfway through this time came "The Oak Brook Moment." My former boss from the transportation industry met with me in Oak Brook, Illinois, and offered me a great package to return. Although it was affirming and flattering, God had not released me from my new position. I give more details of this encounter at the chapter's conclusion, but it's important to note that we face Oak Brook moments and need to be prepared to process opportunities for advancement. Little did I know at the time that God was releasing favor into my future.

Near the end of my initial fourteen months in the health care industry I was planning an exit strategy that was giving me only a fraction of the financial leverage I had gained, but it afforded a way for me to remain true to God's acceptable accounting principles. I had given the new effort my best energies and, for a mere eighty thousand dollars, I was going to leave my newly acquired share of the company. My boss's unexpected death occurred before I sold, and this proved to be a turning point in my financial career. Rather than selling and leaving the company, the atmosphere changed significantly, allowing me to remain.

Let me ask you my young friends, regardless of how the conclusion to your own story will read, can you commit to the following standard by inserting your expertise area? "I will follow God's acceptable _____ principles."

Daniel's Commitment to God's Leadership Principles

In the Old Testament book of Daniel we find a man distinguished among the administrators by his exceptional qualities. King Darius was about to set Daniel over the whole kingdom when others became jealous. These associates are referred to as royal administrators, prefects, satraps, advisors, and governors. They didn't like the king's plans at all. So they schemed to have the king sign a decree that would harm Daniel's reputation (Dan. 6:8). Once a law was written by the Medes and the Persians, it was difficult to reverse. Daniel knew of the decree and continued to honor God by praying anyway; that activity earned him a trip to the lions' den.

Although our pressures may not be life threatening, they can definitely be life altering. Your loyalties will be tested and the qualities of commitment and dedication will create tension at work. What we learn from Daniel, and I trust is fairly represented in my story above, is the importance of remaining true to your commitment to God and his principles in life.

Steps to Maintaining Dedication and Commitment

Sometimes trite advice seems impotent, which leads to one of the dangerous traps in business—ignoring sound suggestions. The basic standards of my accounting profession are well known and sometimes assumed, but not followed. We're all aware of the Enrons of our era.

Around the recent turn of the century, several prominent companies violated generally accepted accounting principles and fraudulently inflated the value of their companies. The same goes with our maturity in other areas, such as spirituality.

Given this scenario, you might find my steps traditional or old school. I ask that you keep in mind that the Latin root for *tradition* implies that which is passed down that is beneficial for the next generation. Simply put, there are some basic rules that are for our own development, and they are timeless.

> *"Keep in mind that the deeper you go spiritually, the more consistent you grow spontaneously."*

1. Establish a prayer routine. Keep in mind that the deeper you go spiritually, the more consistent you grow spontaneously. Many business decisions give little notice and call for split-second decisions. Being in tune with God will help you sense his will.

2. Establish reminders for yourself that God's standards are perfect, and provide added incentives for maintaining professional standards. Remember to insert your profession in a commitment phrase: "I commit to God's acceptable _____ standards."

3. Reflect often on stories of commitment, and recognize they overlap with your own challenges and questions. There are countless examples here, and they become the most helpful when they intersect in some way with your own journey.

4. Set an initial commitment time for a job. Though the corporate world hires and fires weekly, and you'll see amazing numbers of transitions that seem to lessen the need for commitment, make an attempt to stay with a position for a reasonable amount of time. Hang pictures on your wall or photos in your cubicle, and remember, "Wherever you are, be there until you leave."

Stories of Commitment Are Linked to Our Resolve to Persist

One of my story moments came on the battlefield—literally, though the lessons helped in the trenches of daily business deals. I was privileged to attend the sixtieth anniversary of D-day on June 6, 2004. I walked up and down Normandy's beaches for nearly five days, both before, during, and after June 6. Throughout those days, numerous heroic stories surfaced. The dedication of Americans to their role as soldiers and their ultimate commitment to our democracy, literally to you and me, touched me deeply.

A couple of stories reminded me of the possible extent of our human will, far beyond any challenge at work. One young soldier who carried a roll of wire for setting demolition charges had been critically injured by enemy fire. A platoon sergeant summoned the private to bring over his roll of wire while he was still busy in the distance. As the shell-shocked private approached the group he replied, "I will, just as soon as I know what to do with this." In addition to the roll of wire, they suddenly noticed that he was also carrying one of his arms, blown off in a blast moments earlier.

We also were privileged to travel with the actual men who have been depicted in the documentary, *Band of Brothers*. Their sacrifices to remove the German guns from the French Brecourt Manor near St. Mere Eglise saved countless American lives on the landing beaches.

President George W. Bush spoke at the American Cemetery in Collieville Sur-Mer on the anniversary date of June 6. After recounting similar stories of the invasion, and the nine thousand lives represented by the tombstones, he closed by saying, "And we would do it again for our friends."

There will be times when you are giving your best in the management of others and you feel like quitting. The road to success sometimes gets lonely, rough, and risky, but perseverance pays off. The financial gains might be later in the same company after weathering turbulent times, or in another company where your honed skills allow you to excel with more ease. Keep in mind the reasons for taking your current position, and use those reasons to stay motivated for your reasonable training period.

The Three Lights of Moving On

We tend to make job changes for two contrary reasons—escape or advancement.

When you begin to feel like moving on, and as you seek guidance from above, a nautical lesson provides a way to structure this decision. As ships enter a harbor, often through fog and traffic, three lights have to line up to guide them and to give them permission to enter. The navigation lights are located on the shore and must be visible to the harbor pilot at the ship's helm.

Similar to these three lights, the following three principles need to align as we make decisions:

1. Is what you are proposing to do in accordance with the Word of God?

2. Is it in accordance with the leading of the Holy Spirit?

3. Do you have perspective on the circumstances surrounding your decision?

Escape from a particular employment position may be necessary, but don't do so prematurely. You may presently be in a management situation that requires more dedication and commitment than you're prepared for or able to give.

Most business careers have seasons of real struggle. The hours may be long, monetary rewards lacking, and relationships strained or simply unpleasant. Your family may have to live in an area or country deemed unsafe.

You may be forced to be involved in management at a level that makes you uncomfortable. It may be time for you to begin searching for a better tomorrow.

I have learned not to get those three lights, as listed above, out of order. For example, never let the trend of circumstances dictate your major decisions. Circumstances can change very quickly, and without the leading of the Word and the Holy Spirit, you will be like a ship without a rudder.

When I was faced with the Oak Brook moment, I began to get more deeply involved in my Scripture reading and more sensitive to the leading of the Holy Spirit. Although the comparison isn't a true one, I often think of the dark circumstances surrounding our Lord when he was faced with suffering and death, and yet he stayed the course. No, it wasn't a business deal. It was much more important—even more so than the sacrifice at Normandy. However, to separate our business life from our humanity, from our spiritual needs, and from our heritage, is to lose the best chance of perspective.

There are times for advancement. When the three lights align, who are we to say "No" to God after he's honed our skills for more influence and responsibility?

While things were going well while I was working in the transportation business, one phone call had me looking for the lights: "Should I take it? Or, at least, explore it?" I decided to explore it. Maybe this was the leading of the Lord that I had been seeking.

I began testing to see if this was an opportunity worth pursuing. I started taking one-day airplane trips from Ohio to Minnesota in order to determine whether or not I should make the move. I had been offered an accounting position in Minnesota, and I wanted to be sure that the new job would be in accordance with God's will for my life. I did that for several weeks, but I still wasn't sure. Then, I decided to set out a fleece. You know, like Gideon did in the Old Testament (Judg. 6:36–40). Kind of like, "Well, Lord, if this is really you talking to me, then let _____ happen."

My first fleece happened while I was attending a midweek prayer service in our Ohio church. The speaker was from out of town, and I had never heard of him. So, it seemed a perfect time for a fleece. "OK, Lord, if I am to move to Minneapolis, Minnesota, then let the speaker say 'Minneapolis, Minnesota,' in his message tonight." I nearly fell out of the pew when the speaker spoke of just coming from a certain church in Minneapolis, Minnesota. It was so eerie!

Then, just like Gideon, I thought it necessary to test the Lord one more time. The second fleece was perhaps a bit more common, and it involved the sale of our house. I didn't want to place a sign in my yard because I didn't want to unnecessarily alert my current employer. If this opportunity wasn't of the Lord, I would stay where I was. However, my test again received a quick and obvious answer. Within a week a gentleman called me and asked if I knew of any houses for sale in my area of the city! My home sold immediately and within two weeks the negotiations had been completed. These signs were the clincher in making our decision to relocate.

However, only a year later I became uneasy, wondering if I had made the right decision because of the tension with my new boss that I've already described. Though dedicated and committed to my new position, I struggled intensely for a three-month period, rethinking the entire move while seeking the Lord's face through regular fasting and trips to our local denomination's campground. It was a special place in my spiritual upbringing and a place for long serious talks with God. It was at this point that the Oak Brook moment occurred.

Out of the blue a letter came from my previous vice president. He wanted to meet with me the next time I was in the Chicago area. It just so happened that a seminar was scheduled for me in Oak Brook, near his office. The seminar had been scheduled long before his letter arrived.

We met in the VP's office for about two hours prior to the seminar. A plea was made by the company for me to rejoin them as soon as I could. At the close of the meeting, I made the following statement: "I don't know whether or not you will completely understand what I am about to say, but the Lord has not yet revealed to me that I should leave my present job." I excused myself and proceeded across the parking lot to the seminar location.

My immediate thoughts were of how I had just blown a great opportunity. Needless to say, I went to the seminar in somewhat of a depressed state, wondering what the Lord had in mind for my future.

That future was revealed to me about six weeks later when the business partner (who was my superior because he owned more stock in the company, in addition to being the sole owner of some of the businesses we were managing) that I had been at odds with suddenly died of a heart attack. I then knew, without a doubt, that I had taken the new position based on prayer and the Lord had placed me there for a reason. After his death, his personally held businesses went directly to his family, whereas our jointly held business went to me and my other partner.

Commitment and dedication, when surrendered to the Lord, can lead you to heights in management that you only dreamed about. I suddenly found myself at the helm of a major business. Following God's guidance through job transitions had led to an amazing business opportunity in ways I had not imagined.

Questions for Reflection

1. What are the industry standards to which you are committed?

2. Discuss your prayer routines.

3. What have you managed by "signs" and what have you managed by the Word?

4. When does corporate loyalty conflict with Biblical principles?

Additional Resources

Friesen, Garry. *Decision Making and the Will of God* (Sister, Ore.: Multnomah Publishers, 2004).

Peabody, Larry. *Secular Work Is Full-Time Service* (Ft. Washington, Pa.: Christian Literature Crusade, 1974).

Record, B. and R. Singer. *Made to Count: Discovering What to Do with Your Life* (Nashville: W Publishing Group, 2004).

Sherman, Doug and William Hendricks. *Your Work Matters to God* (Colorado Springs: NavPress, 1987).

Sinelli, T. A. *True Riches* (Santa Cruz, Calif.: Lit Torch Publishing, 2001).

4

Doing or Delegating:
Knowing When to Listen or to Let Go

*So now, go. I am sending you to Pharaoh to bring
my people the Israelites out of Egypt.*

–Exodus 3:10

Delegated Duties

Are you willing to delegate? Or, do you think you must handle all the decisions because no one else under you is as qualified? Oftentimes people delay delegation because they can do the job more quickly, yet they find themselves doing the same job the next time it surfaces.

It's not too much of a stretch to find value in the discipleship model utilized by Jesus—regardless of one's religion. Although it's much more than delegation, we find Christ's central plan of disseminating the gospel in Matthew 28; it's known as the Great Commission. We also find the flipside of this in John 6:60–66, a time when some of the disciples left him because of the tough teaching and their implied demands. Jesus does not chase after those he deems not teachable. Regardless of their personalities, position, and giftedness, Jesus realized that he needed to give his energies to those who would carry on his work here on earth. As Christian business men and women we should be all the more attentive to the strategy he used.

Part of the dynamic that takes place through delegation is that it allows for development for both your employee and yourself. The person receiving the assignment may end up doing the task better than you. Consequently, you must swallow your pride and inform him or her how well they did. Though this inherently is the right thing to do, it often results in added dividends for you and the company. For those in smaller businesses, the ability to have others to relieve the pressure of your workload becomes essential for survival. It simultaneously allows you to attend to matters of higher priority and to have time for personal growth strategies. The alternative is a leader squandering strategic time through constant troubleshooting.

Malcolm in the Marketplace

Many of my best lessons came from observing friends' best practices. One of these lessons came from John Bell. He owned a pasteboard-making business based in Marion, Indiana, and he operated several manufacturing plants elsewhere.

John inherited the business at age twenty-eight when his father died. He realized he'd have to assume leadership, and at a young age made a brilliant move.

John called together all his senior managers. They were all several years his senior, averaging fifty-seven years old. He wisely asked for their counsel on how to run all the operations, and also asked for them to tutor him. Together they built a more efficient operation that soon grew well beyond what his father had bequeathed. John was not afraid to delegate. It was a win-win situation for all and, in turn, benefited many charities in our area.

One of the lessons we presented at our business seminars in Elk, Poland, had to do with delegating. The venue was an automobile plant that made wiring harnesses. The plant manager was very enthusiastic and would often interrupt the session for the benefit of his team. When one of our seminar speakers would make a point that the manager felt was important, he would say, "Wait a minute. I want all of my forty managers who are here to make certain they are taking notes on this particular point." As guests in his manufacturing plant, we obliged by pausing our presentation, sometimes much to the chagrin of the remaining seminar participants who were not his employees.

He was exercising leadership at its best by ensuring that the managers under him took on responsibilities and were well trained to do so.

Little did we know (until the seminar was over—it lasted three days) that he had been requiring his managers to stay at work after seminar hours and put into practice all they had learned on that particular day.

Learning from Other Leaders

While delegation is a sign of authority, it's also expected and should represent sound decision making. It becomes a sign of effective leadership. But good leadership needs to follow good advice as well. Where do you go for such guidance?

Our firm was getting ready to expand into the state of Indiana. We were heavily involved in the field of health care at the time and I wanted to discover what had to be done to successfully operate in that state. After contacting the State Health Care Association that covered our industry, I learned the names of successful operators. Then I went about contacting them and asked for a meeting at their convenience. To my surprise, several responded favorably to me. Subsequently, I knew what our firm needed to do to excel—learn from the best practices of these successful administrators. In a sense, I wanted to follow the footprints of successful managers.

Learning from Robinson Crusoe

The story of Robinson Crusoe has amazed millions for years. It is so extraordinary that most consider it fantasy. However, it's historical fiction. That is, it's based on the true stories of a real live Robinson Crusoe.[1] His actual name was Alexander Selkirk (1676–1721) and the story has been detailed in works such as Robert Kraske's *Marooned: The Strange but True Adventures of Alexander Selkirk*.[2] And it is almost certain that before the London author, Daniel Defoe, wrote the novel of *Robinson Crusoe*, he met up with Selkirk.

Alexander Selkirk was born in Scotland. He was a mariner by trade, but considered by many to be a rather strange man. We don't know the reason why, but perhaps for some sociological experiment, Selkirk had himself marooned on an island off the coast of Chile.

He arranged for the captain of a ship to set him off on the small island of Masa-Teaerra, where he lived alone for nearly five years. The captain of the ship was to return and retrieve him on a precise day, which he did. The unfortunate thing about the experiment was that when Selkirk was retrieved, he could not speak. It took some time for his mind to be healed from those several years of solitary confinement. With the help of the crew, he was able to regain his vocabulary and speech. He never fully adjusted again to civilization and spent much of the rest of his life in a cave in Scotland. He eventually returned to the sea at age forty-five and apparently died of scurvy.

Although the parallel to the Robinson Crusoe story is incomplete, Selkirk's story was indeed its impetus. After Selkirk's island adventure, Richard Steele interviewed him for *The Englishman* and Europe became aware of this amazing venture, a story Daniel Defoe consulted for his classic Crusoe adventures and one surfacing in a wide array of texts including Charles Dickens' *The Pickwick Papers*.

In Defoe's account, Crusoe was shipwrecked on what he thought was an uninhabited island. Much like Tom Hanks' character in the modern movie *Cast Away,* Crusoe survived through his own ingenuity. He hunted, crafted clothes, planted foodstuffs, and more than subsisted. He actually came to enjoy the experience.

When he was finally discovered and rescued, he was not a recluse like Alexander Selkirk; instead he wanted to tell everybody of his experience. He was a fine Christian man in the story and he wanted to speak of God's goodness during those years of isolation on that island.

The basic difference between the historical account of Alexander Selkirk and the modified account of Robinson Crusoe was a footprint he noticed in the sand. Crusoe had observed cannibals occasionally landing on his island and having a gory feast, with plenty of bones left to confirm his suspicions. On one of those occasions when he went down to inspect the bones, he saw a footprint in the sand leading away to another part of the island. First terrified, then mystified, he could not rest until he found whose footprint it was and he followed it until he came upon a man. On that Friday he found the man and named him "My Man Friday." In Defoe's story, Crusoe leads this man to Christ, and they eventually return to civilization and live together as life-long friends.

Before we segue back to the business world, keep in mind that the lesson from Crusoe is pregnant with help. He followed a footprint. In doing so, he took the initiative. Also, as the story unfolds, he realizes that though some conversations and events prove tough, he still needs Friday's advice, help, and companionship.

Adjusting to Uneven Paths

The road of managing can sometimes get rocky and risky, and it can become a lonely one. When your road gets rocky, then is the time for you to begin consulting your Senior Partner, God himself, in earnest. Hopefully, you will have been consulting him all along. However, we have all faced our share of rocky times that finally drove us to our knees.

As I'm nearing the end of my career, younger business men and women only see the security I have from past investments, but they don't see the many times I had to look for footprints.

There was a time in our operations that we were facing a cut in revenue of 19 percent. That's right! Nineteen! That kind of action can put one into bankruptcy rather quickly. What could we do? We assembled all our top managers and held a conference with them at an away-from-the-office place. I wanted them to begin to dream about how we could overcome the hand we had been dealt so that we could survive. I wanted them to be able to concentrate solely on the circumstances at hand.

Believe it or not, we devised plans on how to reduce expenses and continue giving adequate service. Many people, including senior management, had to take cutbacks. We survived. Thankfully, the reduction in revenue did not last forever, and we were able to get back on an even keel. Our Senior Partner had been invited to the meeting and we appreciated the wisdom that he gave in that troubling hour. Keep in mind that we should always seek the footprints that lead not just to a man named Friday, but to our God who guides us on our way.

The road can also get risky at times, and may occur in several different ways. Again, reach out for counsel, and don't try to solve all the problems yourself. There is help available. For example, my company had the opportunity to purchase a business that was in bankruptcy. After wise counsel we purchased it and turned it into a financially profitable venture. On another occasion, we searched for businesses to acquire, and in doing so also learned which ones to pass by.

Leaders will lead and managers will manage when the going gets rough and rocky. You cannot go it alone. If you attempt to go it alone, you may end up like Alexander Selkirk. His fate came as a result of his own actions to distance himself from others. Don't fall into that trap. There are people available to assist you, and—believe it or not—they don't all charge a fee for their services. Help is available for the asking. Begin with your Senior Partner and allow him to direct your footsteps to other sources. When one does this, the road becomes less rocky and considerably less lonely.

A set of footprints that I had the privilege of following were those of a plant manager. I was a young manager under his command. When I would go to his office to discuss management problems, I always knew exactly what my assignments were when I left his presence. In fact, he would not only verbally recap the meeting, he would also follow up with a memo that would state exactly what he was going to do as a result of the meeting. He also included what I was expected to do. That method of management has shaped me to the present.

The Lessons of Nehemiah

When Nehemiah, who was in Persian captivity, learned that the wall of his city, Jerusalem, was still torn down and its gates burned, he was downcast. One day, King Artaxerxes of Persia noticed Nehemiah's countenance. After learning of Jerusalem's plight, the king allowed Nehemiah to take a leave of absence in order to take care of the business of restoring the wall and gates.

Nehemiah arrived in Jerusalem and quickly sized up the situation. He immediately planned his work and then promptly set about working his plan. He notified all of his colleagues of the seriousness of the matter, and they followed his lead.

Each man working on the wall was ordered to keep his weapon nearby, just in case an attack occurred from known enemies in the area. In fact, Nehemiah said, "neither I nor my brothers nor my men nor the guards with me took off our clothes" (Neh. 4:23).

"He immediately planned his work and then promptly set about working his plan."

For fifty-two days this went on, and the wall was completed and the gates were hung. Talk about dedication. Talk about commitment—all credited to Nehemiah's superb leadership.

Nehemiah did not spend time wandering around, wringing his hands, and saying, "Oh, woe is me. What will we do?" No, he exercised leadership and took charge. The people followed his instructions because Nehemiah got busy and set the example.

Leader or Wanderer— Which Will It Be for You?

Perhaps it's fitting to end this section with the great story of Moses. He had his hands full attempting to lead millions of Israelites from Egypt to Canaan, across waters, deserts, and mountains. They weren't always cooperative with Moses' leadership style, and he was exhausted after trying to do everything himself. He wanted to do all the leading and call all the shots all the time. He apparently didn't know the meaning of the word delegate.

In the book of Exodus, we find Moses providing, with God's help, food, water, and safety, but the followers still were discontent. They had just come to a watering hole and had their thirst quenched, but the people were quarrelling so badly among themselves that they named the place *Meribah,* meaning "argument and strife." They were certainly a bunch of unhappy campers, to say the least. Well, Moses wasn't helping the situation any because he was trying to solve all the problems by himself. The poor guy was working 24/7 trying to figure out how to assemble an army to fight as well as taking on all the other responsibilities of civic management.

He grew so tired trying to fulfill all his duties, that some of his men had to prop up his hands during an ensuing battle with the army of Amalek because Moses just wasn't up to the task. Perhaps you or I couldn't have done better, but Moses was lacking one very important ingredient: he was failing to delegate.

This failure happens to too many leaders and managers. They would rather do it themselves than take the time to teach some of their subordinates how to share in the duties.

Enter Jethro, Moses' father-in-law. Like any decent and worthwhile father-in-law, Jethro had heard of Moses' successes and wanted to come to see what it was all about. Now, it is interesting to note here that Jethro brought his daughter, Zipporah, Moses' wife, with him. The book tells us that Moses had sent her home some time before. Ever wonder why he did that? Perhaps it was because she didn't have much of a home life, with Moses spending all his time settling disputes, fighting wars, looking for food and water, and the like. It's quite possible that Moses was so wrapped up in tending to Israel's needs that he was neglecting his family big time. Now, Zipporah returns, along with their two sons.

When Jethro arrived, Moses first asked him about his health. It seems they hadn't seen each other for a while since Moses had to update Jethro on what had been happening from the time they had left Egypt until the present. Then, Moses began to express his problems to Jethro.

The next day, Jethro went about watching Moses at work. His observation: "What is this you are doing for the people? Why do you alone sit as judge, while all these people stand around you from morning till evening?" (Ex. 18:14).

Moses told him that the people kept coming to him with their disputes and to ask for advice. He was their judge and decided who was right and wrong and instructed them in God's ways (see Ex. 18:15–16).

Now, if you look at this closely, Moses was not only making a quick decision on who was right or wrong, but he was also conducting classes with each one who came. Wow! Talk about time consuming! No wonder he was never home; he was spending too much time at the "office."

Jethro told Moses that this wasn't right. Moses was going to wear himself out if he kept this up. This job was too heavy a burden for Moses to handle by himself (see Ex. 18:18).

So Jethro, who was apparently well-versed in management, put Moses in the front row of the seminar and began to lecture him. Jethro said, "Listen now to me and I will give you some advice, and may God be with you. You must be the people's representative before God and bring their disputes to him. Teach them the decrees and laws, and show them the way to live and the duties they are to perform" (Ex. 18:19–20).

Now listen carefully, to Jethro's central point: he wanted Moses to find some capable, godly, honest men who hated bribes. Moses was to appoint them as judges with one judge for each one thousand people. There will be ten judges under him, each in charge of a hundred; and under each of them will be two judges, each responsible for the affairs of fifty people, and each of those judges will have five judges beneath him, each counseling ten people (see Ex. 18:21).

Jethro went on to say, "Have them serve as judges for the people at all times, but have them bring every difficult case to you; the simple cases they can decide themselves. That will make your load lighter, because they will share it with you" (Ex. 18:22).

Finally, Jethro told Moses that if he followed this advice, he would be able to endure the pressures, and there would be peace and harmony in the camp (see Ex. 18:23).

Then a miracle happened: Moses heard and followed his father-in-law's advice. Moses then organized his people in leadership positions and removed the burden from himself.

My Ultimate Decision Has Been My Most Serious Business

A man came along one day and put his footprints on the sandy seashore of my life and said, "Follow me." His footprints were nail-scarred. His name is Jesus of Nazareth. I began to follow him and have been following him ever since. It has made all the difference in my life.

I've never regretted it. Many have left their footprints on my life, but none like his. I am now never alone. The rocky places have been smoothed out. Now, I always have someone I can confide in—even when no one else is around.

Who is putting footprints on your life? Are they footprints that are designed to elevate you? Will they make you a better person? Are they footprints that will lead you forever upward? If so, those are the footprints that will count for time and eternity.

Questions for Reflection

1. What strategies can you use to assist in the development of your employees?

2. Even when you are tempted to go it alone, why would it be helpful for you to seek advice?

3. How easy is it for you to learn from the successes of others?

4. Why is it so important to be willing to delegate?

5. How quickly do you adjust to uneven paths?

Additional Resources

Briner, Robert A. *The Management Methods of Jesus* (Nashville: Thomas Nelson, 1996).

Briner, Bob and Ray Pritchard. *The Leadership Lessons of Jesus: A Timeless Model for Today's Leaders* (Nashville: Broadman and Holman, 1998).

Covey, Stephen R. *The Seven Habits of Highly Effective People: Powerful Lessons in Personal Change* (New York: Simon and Schuster, 1995).

Pope, S. *The Manager's Pocket Guide to Team Sponsorship* (Amherst, Mass.: HRD Press, 1998).

Zigarelli, M. *Ordinary People Extraordinary Leaders* (Gainsville, Fla.: Synergy Publishers, 2002).

5

Feed the Good Horses Well

So in everything, do to others what you would have them do
to you, for this sums up the Law and the Prophets.
—Matthew 7:12

The Herzberg Principle

Jerry Pattengale, my friend, has traveled the country emphasizing a purpose-guided approach to learning and leadership. One key element of his view relates directly to my principle, "feed the good horses well." On the surface, it seems simple enough and perhaps reflects my age—still thinking of the days when teams of strong horses were used on farms.

Lean into this analogy and look at what research has uncovered about workplace dynamics. The essence of noted psychologist Frederick Herzberg's *Motivator-Hygiene* theory is that keeping workers satisfied doesn't necessarily make them motivated.[1] His article on this subject became the most requested reprint by *The Harvard Business Review*, surpassing a million requests.[2] Let me explain.

In his studies, Herzberg's found that workers were listing a series of dissatisfactions with their work environment. Managers were addressing those concerns, and in time removed them. However, a startling result occurred. These same employees weren't necessarily satisfied, just no longer dissatisfied! So instead of finding more successful employees he found more non-dissatisfied employees. The areas of dissatisfaction were mainly those related to extrinsic factors and not linked to intrinsic motivation. In other words, they may be frustrated with the copy machine, parking or a particular policy, but these matters were not associated with anything that was part of their personal life goals or even among their vested insterests.

The study helps us in another way. Herzberg discovered that the non-dissatisfaction areas were all tied to extrinsic (external) motivation to tangible items. These are not attached to the employees' intrinsic (internal) motivation, the most crucial element for sustained performance. It takes both extrinsic and intrinsic values for employees to succeed in the workplace, but intrinsic motivation is the most potent.

The following illustration portrays how our company successfully employed extrinsic motivation, but our goodwill seemed to strike a chord with their intrinsic motivation—a desire to please managers who were attempting to establish a great work environment.

Malcolm in the Marketplace

Every fifth year, our company held its annual convention in the beautiful state of Hawaii. We set up an incentive plan for each of our senior managers. If they met the goals, they and their spouses would attend the convention with all expenses paid. The convention was four days long, with a few added days at the beginning or at the end for an extra vacation. After all, sitting through seminars on a daily basis between the prime hours of 8 a.m. and 5 p.m. in a place as beautiful as Hawaii, got a little monotonous.

Offering these incentives was our method of rewarding our "good horses." They rewarded the organization by actually paying their own way through their additional effort in winning the contest. In the end we received better, more conscientious managers. Soon the word spread to other similar organizations and we became the employer of choice.

Later on, we arranged a similar contest that included all our employees. Each facility selected an Employee of the Year. Then all of the Employees of the Year competed for the grand prize of Grand Employee of the Year. That person was given a full week's vacation, with pay, to one of several destinations, including Hawaii. They could also take along a companion at our cost. Oh, yes, they also received five hundred dollars for traveling money.

When those employees returned, word quickly spread about the great time they had. Needless to say, that created quite a stir among our employees because they all wanted to go the following year. The criteria was simple. For the Employee of the Year, they were judged on attitude, appearance, absenteeism, loyalty, and cooperation.

The following year many of our employees received an "A" in each of the above criteria. The Grand Employee of the Year was chosen by each facility's managerial staff, from that particular facility's Employees of the Year program. Next, an essay was written by each of the employees about why they thought they should be the winner. It was all forwarded to our corporate office for final selection.

When employees are treated as the greatest resource that the business possesses, those same employees will respond in a positive manner.

There were times when pay raises were given to our employees much to the detriment of the organization's stockholders. Did it jeopardize our business to do so? No, but the stockholders had to settle for a little less each time we did that. It was beneficial to our employees because it struck a chord with them internally and intrinsic motivation began to grow through this open display of our company's commitment to them.

We wanted our employees to be rewarded for all their efforts and this was simply one of the methods we used to do just that. We began to create a family atmosphere in our organizations that assisted us greatly when we were looking for additional employees. While similar companies struggled to find employees, we had no problem in doing so.

I recall one year when the recipient of the Grand Employee of the Year was employed at one of our Ohio facilities, and he won a full-week trip to Hawaii. My wife and I arrived at the Indianapolis airport just before the employee's flight was to depart. The surprise and appreciation on his face was priceless. Our gesture was taken for what it was—a personal statement about his worth and about our excitement for him.

We had chosen to feed our good horses well, or in this case, one of our grandest employees. We reaped a tremendous amount of goodwill from that employee in the months and years to come.

The Joseph Approach

The book of Genesis describes Joseph's rise to power. After he interpreted Pharaoh's dream, Pharaoh called his assistants together and asked for input in appointing someone as manager of a nationwide farm program. Pharaoh asked them if they knew someone who could do it better than Joseph (see Gen. 48:37).

Pharaoh then appointed Joseph to manage the entire project. Joseph's orders would reveberate throughout Egypt. The only person to outrank Joseph was the Pharaoh (see Gen. 41:40). The endorsement was strengthened even further when he placed a signet ring on Joseph's finger as a token of his authority.

They dressed Joseph in beautiful clothing and had a royal golden chain placed around his neck. In effect, all the major credit cards of the kingdom were given to him. Likewise, Joseph received a chariot, demonstrating he was second in command throughout the entire land. The pharaoh's endorsement was also manifested publicly with the gift of a wife to Joseph, one from a prestigious family. He had awesome responsibility and the authority to match.

Joseph had it all, and he was ready to go to work. A big task lay ahead and he knew it. First, he surveyed the land. After all, if they were going to have seven good years of prosperity before seven bad years of famine, he needed to get started to maximize the acreage with bountiful crops.

Pharaoh recognized Joseph's abilities and offered him everything necessary to accomplish the task. And as the Bible outlines, Joseph was successful in protecting Egypt during times of famine. From this account, two key management principles emerge:

1. Give authority commensurate with responsibility.
2. Employees' response is usually commensurate with employers' treatment.

Many managers practice a corrupted form of the Golden Rule. That is, "He who has the gold makes the rules." That may sound cute, but in reality, the results will be negative. It's not a stretch to assume poor working relationships and morale in such an environment.

Angels and Mortals

A few weeks before Christmas each of our facilities sponsored a program called "Angels and Mortals." In this scheme, each employee was simultaneously both an angel and a mortal. That is, they were an angel to another employee—the mortal. The object was for the angel to do nice things for their particular mortal anonymously such as attach notes on timecards, put candy at the mortal's workstation, send nice cards, and so forth.

A couple of days before Christmas, all angels and mortals would be gathered together and the employees had to attempt to identify their angel. This created a tremendous amount of good feeling between all staff, especially between managers and employees. Pleasant memories lasted several weeks, and it was difficult for employees with otherwise sour dispositions to remain so.

I've discovered through decades of overseeing a wide variety of employees that some tend to have an undue share of negative traits. It is sometimes more difficult to find their real value. It's usually there, but just buried a bit deeper. Like mining for gold, we may need to sift through tons of gravel in order to get to it. Positive acts on our part, however, usually get us there.

What kind of manager are you? How do you treat your employees? With respect? Or do you treat them as someone whom you hired just to help achieve your goals? How do you want to be treated? What if Christ's Golden Rule were applied to you?

Signs of the Times: Opening Doors for Your Staff

There is a rather successful business in my city named Signs of the Times, founded by a woman with an amazing work ethic. If she were to place signs on the doors of the businesses she serves, indicating their management style and character, how would they read? What sign would appear on your door?

Pause a minute and ask yourself what sign would your employees post on your door? "Open only during posted hours" or "Enter only at great risk." Perhaps signs that say "Closed" or "Sorry." Or, maybe it would be something along the lines of "Welcome" or, "If I'm not here, call my cell."

We could stretch this analogy quite a bit, examining the doors themselves, from doors that swing both ways to the appearance and construction of the doors. However, perhaps one historic note will serve us well here, and it relates to the patterns on our nation's early colonial doors. The upper half of the door resembles a cross, and the lower half an open Bible.

With this in mind, think again about the signs that would be posted on such a door to your office. Also, think about your office habits. If your office door is always closed, the message you are sending is "Stay out." If partially open, the message is, "Knock before you enter, but it must be very important." If half open, then you may be saying, "Enter, if necessary." If completely open, then your message is, "Enter anytime you wish."

What kind of a door are you? What makes you unique? I always enjoyed working with managers who maintained a completely open door, and I felt comfortable interrupting them if necessary. I usually left their office having gained direction, and sometimes encouragement or inspiration.

Creating Open Doors among Employees

During our Ethics in Business seminars in the Eastern Bloc countries during the 1990s, we encountered a rather cold environment among workers. Participants were eager to learn, but they were not anxious to get to know one another even though they had lived in the same community for many years.

We attempted to dissolve those barriers by using several different methods, but the real dangers they experienced under Communist rule created tension. Neighbor informed on neighbor, and sometimes for simple material gains. Many of the participants entered the seminar as loners and hoped to stay that way.

Using a hologram exercise, we were able to prompt interaction between participants. Pictures of the Eiffel Tower, Statue of Liberty, and an exotic airplane were tacked to the wall, and one could see in three dimensions if you knew how to focus your eyes to make it happen.

"An effective manager will attempt to create an atmosphere in the workplace that makes everyone feel comfortable."

Our method was to show one person how to see the picture in 3-D, and then let that person show others how to do it. They were so excited to learn how to see the picture in 3-D, that they quickly responded by showing the next person in line. In this manner, they began to communicate with each other.

An effective manager will attempt to create an atmosphere in the workplace that makes everyone feel comfortable. It is the manager's responsibility to learn of any barriers that keep employees from working together. Learn to treat employees as family.

Mr. C. William Pollard of Service Master notes, "Service Master is well-known for its commitment to high ethical standards and strongly encourages the employees to uphold them. We recognize the value of each person as being created in the image of God. Every individual, regardless of intelligence, background, race or position has great dignity and intrinsic worth." This reflects closely the Service Master's official Financial Code of Ethics as approved in 2004.[3]

We will all be held accountable before God for how we go about conducting our business, and for how we treat our employees.

Jesus tells us that when we give, we will receive, "a good measure, pressed down, shaken together and running over" (Luke 6:38). He goes on to say that whatever measure we use to give—large or small—will be used to measure what is given back to us.

Many times this passage is used to relate giving to money or assets. We can also interpret it to mean giving of things other than those of monetary value. Do you want a large measure to be given to you? Then give in large measures and you will find this passage of his Word is true. Such giving can mean the giving of kindness and consideration as well as respect. Showing kindness and respect to an employee will have its own reward.

A Business Lesson from Missionaries

A few years ago, I was advising a missionary organization on how they could maximize a property they owned in California. The property had been used as a birthing center for unwed mothers and was no longer needed for that purpose.

My first thought was to attempt to turn it into an assisted living facility and an apartment complex to serve their own constituents. I asked a friend in the California health care business to meet me at the complex to assist in the decision making.

While going through the complex, we came upon a lovely couple who had just retired from spending forty years on the mission field in Africa. We engaged them in conversation because they were living in the facility on a temporary basis and we wanted to learn about that arrangement.

The couple relayed their experiences of being in a foreign country and serving there as missionaries for such a long period of time. They proudly shared about their two sons who were now serving mankind in another capacity. Whereupon, my friend asked, "Don't you have many regrets of having spent most of your life in a foreign country on a mission field?" To which the couple replied, "Regrets? No, we have no regrets at all. In fact, it was a privilege for us to serve."

As we walked away and were commenting about our conversation with the couple, my friend stated, "I wonder who is the richer?" He was feeling it was the missionary couple and not himself who possessed the greater riches. Mother Teresa shared that "the miracle is not that we choose to serve, but that we choose to serve with joy." Proverbs 11:24 says, "One man gives freely, yet gains even more."

Planting Business Seeds:
Working Potato Fields with David Longaberger

I grew up in Conesville, Ohio, and learned a work ethic at an early age. My great uncle owned a potato patch. Well, it was more than a patch; it was several hundred acres. He grew potatoes and sold them to potato chip factories. During harvest time, both he and a potato farmer neighbor would employ children from about the ages of ten through high school age. I worked hard and earned enough money to buy my school clothes, plus extra for expenses during the school year.

One of my potato-picking chums was from a nearby town called Dresden. His name was Dave Longaberger and we called him Popeye because he could screw up his face and mimic the comic strip guy. Dave was among the best at doing the back-breaking work for countless hours, though occasional potato fights relieved some of the tension.

In later years, I would take my children to Dresden where Dave owned and operated Popeye's, a successful restaurant known for its ice cream. He had many innovative ideas on how a restaurant should be run. One of his many customer-oriented policies was to have all the coffee pots emptied every twenty minutes in order to make certain there was always fresh coffee on hand, an innovation way ahead of Starbucks.

Dave later started a business called Longaberger Baskets. That business was a spin-off from something his dad had started several years previously. Longaberger Baskets are known almost world-wide for their quality. Dave was one of those entrepreneurs who was always dreaming of how to make a better product. He not only dreamed it, he lived it, and was able to see the fulfillment of many of his dreams.

Dave had many creative ideas on how to treat his employees. For example, when an employee came to work, they were assigned a specific basket to make. If they didn't want to make that particular one, Dave would give them a few minutes to attempt to trade off with a coworker. He wanted his basket makers to be reasonably happy in what they were doing. He knew this would not only produce a better employee, but it would also produce a better basket.

When we managers learn how to take care of our good horses we end up being the richer.

Questions for Reflection

1. When making decisions affecting employees, how will you get their input?

2. What types of incentives will you provide employees to encourage them?

3. How will you react when other employees receive a bonus of promotion?

4. Where do you turn for advice when the going gets tough?

5. How will you model an open door policy for your employees?

Additional Resources

Crane, Christopher A. and Mike Hamel. *Executive Influence: Impacting Your Workplace for Christ* (Colorado Springs: NavPress, 2003).

Doering, Jeanne. *The Encouragers: Discovering Your Ministry of Affirmation* (Chappaqua N.Y.: Christian Herald Books, 1982).

Maxwell, John C. *The 21 Indispensable Qualities of a Leader: Becoming the Person Others Will Want to Follow* (Nashville: Thomas Nelson, 1999).

Maxwell, John C. and Les Parrott. *25 Ways to Win with People: How to Make Others Feel Like a Million Bucks* (Nashville: Thomas Nelson, 2005).

Rush, Myron. *Management: A Biblical Approach* (Wheaton, Ill.: Victor Books, 1983).

6

Expect the Unexpected

One day when Job's sons and daughters were feasting and drinking wine at the oldest brother's house, a messenger came . . .

–Job 1:13

During the stock market crash in 1987 some of our associates experienced some remarkable financial disasters, much more than my personal losses. For some, the downturn was personally devastating and even ended in suicide. The unexpected loss was more than they could bear.

I learned early on never to invest more than I can afford to lose. Invest wisely so you don't lose sleep over the risks. It's one thing to leverage—which I don't recommend—it's another to take sustained risks. Keep in mind that market changes are way beyond our control, but we can control how much we change, that is, whether we take risks or remain conservative.

One of our young friends, Rob Swagger, is a former vice president for investing at UBS, the largest wealth management firm in the world, and is the president of Veriana Networks, Inc. It's common to hear him give advice to clients, whether old family friends managing modest investments or large project managers of tens of millions: "Be sure to worry about downside protection." That is, expect the unexpected.

Malcolm in the Marketplace

I assisted two of our administrators in purchasing one of the facilities from our operations so that they could personally own and operate facilities. They had raised their investment money and found two other persons to join them in the venture. These new investors had to invest more money than the two administrators.

The money was supplied and the facility was transferred, with the two administrators being the controlling stockholders. As sometimes happens, the day came when one of the two latecomers decided that since he had invested more money than either of the two original stockholders, he should become the principal stockholder.

If the new investor's rationale were true, then anyone who had invested more money than the original stockholders in a business could someday lay claim to become the principal stockholder. For example, many of you reading this book may have more money in Microsoft stocks than Bill Gates used to start his company, but you'd not think to call him for a partnership, let alone principal position. Naturally, latecomers often invest much more than the original stockholder.

Although the four stockholders had been extremely close friends, a lawsuit was filed on the matter. Greed is the primary motivator in many business transactions, and that is why it is so important to operate by the Book.

I sat with the two original stockholders many hours in law firms in the state capital where the facility purchase had been made. In the end, right prevailed over wrong and the investor who had filed the lawsuit was given his investment money back. However, he missed out on a sweet deal, because a few years later the facility was sold and his investment would have more than tripled.

During the time period of the lawsuit, I often used an illustration of successful management with the original stockholders. During my many trips, we would hold brief management meetings at various cafés. On a few occasions, I used the reverse side of a placemat to make my point clear. I used the principle that if you can see something in print or picture form, one will remember what was said for a much longer time. On this particular occasion I had placed several Xs in a zigzag motion on the sheet of paper beginning at the bottom of the page and ending at the top. I then drew a line beginning with the first X to each of the others in a zigzag pattern in order to make my point.

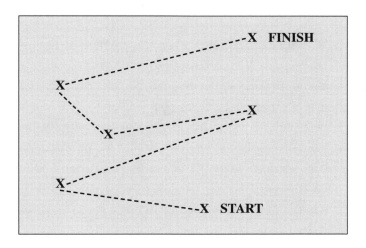

The X at the bottom denotes the beginning; the X at the top denotes the finish. Successful management does not mean that all steps taken have positive results. However, much can be learned through the various steps to avoid setbacks. The zigzag lines illustrated that some efforts would result in taking three steps forward and then two backward, but the final result would be a winning one for the two stockholders. Their attorneys had advised them that the lawsuit was frivolous and contrary to law.

Those two gentlemen took that illustration to heart and began to look optimistically towards the final goal. One of them would often quote the verse that "no weapon forged against you will prevail" (Isa. 54:17). While this might not be used as intended, they took it in the right spirit. They had come face to face with man's fallen nature. In this context, it's important to remember the adage, "There, but for the grace of God go I." That is, business occurs among people constantly tempted to make decisions for selfish reasons; as Christians we're not immune from these temptations. One's theology begins to inform one's analysis of such matters. Whether a business associate backslides (as Wesleyans would say) or is simply disobedient for a season (as the Reformed-minded might say), it still results in hard and tangible financial realities.

A Job Reminder about the Down Side

It's common to hear about the biblical character of Job when life gets tough—whether it's personal or professional, and especially when it's both. We'll look more closely at Job in a minute, but pause to think about how much a serious problem at work—whether it's in relationships or in the ledger books—affects your life at home. Unlike the Old Testament days, we have various legal ways today to keep our business finances separate from our personal finances though one can only lose so much at work before there is none to take home.

Just as we strive to make decisions on principle and not personality (matters of good business), and to separate personal from professional (matters of ethics), we also need to keep our assessment of our worth before God separate from our financial worth. While I've shared here that my relationship with God helped guide me through my business life, and still does, it also helped to sustain me in times of unexpected, and oftentimes, unavoidable losses.

One of Jerry's friends in California literally lost millions of dollars overnight when a fire took one of his main properties. He was in the middle of bringing it up to code when he discovered a violation, the need for concrete or fire retardant shingles, and then the fire came over the San Bernardino range and took his buildings in a matter of minutes. He had given generously to his local church and helped many in missions. It just didn't seem to make sense, and like Job, he went through a time of deep reflection. He also happened to be in a time of expansion and this one uninsured loss started a domino effect. He went from owning a palatial estate and several residences to having none in a matter of months. And like Job, he certainly discovered who his friends were, and more importantly, a refreshing sense of who God is. I'll finish this story later, but first let's turn to Job.

The Bible informs us that Job was an innocent man. In a conversation with Satan, God said that Job was the finest man in all the earth. He was a good man who feared God and wanted nothing to do with evil (see Job 1:8).

Job was going about his business, and business was apparently very good—almost storybook fashion. He was also an exemplary father and his family gathered regularly for special occasions. It was on one such occasion that calamity struck, and fortunately Job was not present. It's at this very point in his life, with a large crowd gathered, that he experienced loss on many fronts. It wasn't private, but very public. Just as we've been discussing, when he least expected it, major challenges occurred in almost every area of life.

Satan attempted to convince God to turn his back on Job (see Job 1:6–12 and 2:1–6). First, Job heard from a frantic messenger that his oxen had been plowing with the donkeys feeding beside them when the Sabeans attacked, drove away the animals, and killed all the farm hands except the one who fled to find Job. Job lost his investments and employees to competitors.

While this messenger was still speaking, another arrived with more bad news: the fire of God had fallen from heaven and burned the sheep and all the herdsmen. Only the messenger escaped. He lost investments and employees to what insurance companies once called an "act of God."

Before this messenger finished, still another messenger rushed in and told Job that three bands of Chaldeans drove off the camels and killed the servants. This messenger was the only one to escape. Job lost more investments and employees.

As this messenger was still speaking, another came and informed Job that his sons and daughters were feasting in their oldest brother's home when a mighty wind swept in from the desert. The wind engulfed the house so that the roof fell in on them. They were all dead. He lost his children to another "act of God."

All this calamity befell Job in the space of a very short time. All that he owned, including his children, had suddenly been taken away. When he thought the loss was great, it became greater. He lost all his worldly possessions and his family.

The question naturally arises: why do bad things happen to good people? Like Jerry's California friend and, in a sense like all of us, it's an appropriate question, and one that consumed Job's life for a season.

Still the unexpected calamities continued. When Job thought the loss was complete, he lost his health. If Job had cursed God and turned his back, he would have also lost much more—not only his own life or self-worth, but also his future blessings!

You're likely familiar with his triumph over his friends' advice and his steadfastness with God. Also, you may recall that in the end he became even wealthier than before the trials came. God is indeed faithful. Regardless of our losses, we need to trust in him and have confidence in our future.

The California businessman also rebounded. With the shifting real estate market, his financial savvy has helped him over the past decade to amass considerable holdings. And, by his own admission, he has done so with much more humility than when he was in his thirties. He now has a much more vibrant ministry of giving.

The unexpected may come to your marketplace. Even in my seventies I realize that my wife and I are not exempt from misfortune. Yes, like most snowbirds we invest much more conservatively. We aren't interested in the large risks, no matter how promising. However, we've both certainly learned not to attempt to do it all on our own power. We seek a Higher Power on a daily basis. You might say that we're going through that season of life where an "act of God" is hitting our bodies—it's called aging. With knee surgeries and related health visits, we're very aware of the unexpected in all facets of life. As in the financial world, when such times come to us we feel the same pain as others, but we also have a sense of ourselves and our God, and we're confident about the future.

Helen Steiner Rice and the Unexpected

In many ways, Helen Steiner Rice is an example of what great ideas and a great business plan can do. The fact that her name is a household word among my generation reflects not only her writing talent, but also her marketing savvy. She captures the sense of personal tragedy with the words of her poem, "The Bend in the Road."

> When we feel we have nothing left to give,
> And we are sure that the "song has ended"—
> When our day seems over and the shadows fall
> And the darkness of night has descended.
> Where can we go to find the strength
> To valiantly keep on trying.
> Where can we find the hand that will dry
> The tears that the heart is crying—
> There's but one place to go and that is to God
> And dropping all pretense and pride,
> We can pour out our problems without restraint
> And gain strength with Him at our side—
> And together we stand at life's crossroads
> And view what we think is the end,
> But God has a much bigger vision
> And He tells us it's only a bend—
> For the road goes on and is smoother,
> And the "pause" in the song is a "rest,"
> And the part that's unsung and unfinished
> Is the sweetest and richest and best—

So rest and relax and grow stronger,
Let go and let God share your load,
Your work is not finished or ended,
You've just come to a "bend in the road."

Helen was well aware of the unexpected. Her father, whom she loved dearly, passed away when she was only twelve years old. She would later marry a banker who gave her a Cinderella-type existence. They enjoyed a mansion, large accounts, and access to most of what this life offers. There's nothing sinister about it; he just made excellent financial decisions. Well, almost. When the stock market crashed in 1929, he lost his fortune and, like some others during that period, committed suicide. Through all that tragedy Helen began to reach out to God. With the support of some of her friends she began to develop her "birthright gift"—her ability to express herself in writing.[1] She honed this gift, and like the above poem, wrote the following poem, "Give Lavishly," as well—among thousands of others. (The emphasis is mine.)

The more you give, the more you get,
The more you laugh, the less you fret,
The more you do unselfishly,
The more you live abundantly.
The more of everything you share,
The more you'll always have to spare.
The more you love, the more you'll find,
That life is good and friends are kind,
For what we give away,
Enriches us from day to day.

When we expect the unexpected, we realize that loss comes in many ways. We also know that like Job, God holds our future as well. And like Helen Steiner Rice, we have birthright gifts that God has given us that we can hone to have influence and to contribute in productive ways. As business men and women, we have the knowledge to rebound. We also have the foreknowledge to prepare as best we can for such occasions.

Questions for Reflection

1. How will you deal with unexpected bad news when it comes your way?

2. What will you do if your company that you have labored long and hard for is suddenly sold?

3. If an economic downturn happens, what will that mean for your business operations?

4. Are you ready to make an unexpected transfer should your situation dictate it?

5. What about unexpected good news?

6. An unexpected promotion comes. What will that mean for you?

7. A sizeable bonus is dropped in your lap. What will you do with it?

8. That supervisor that seemingly always had it in for you has been transferred. So, what does this mean for you?

9. How does the concept of a Silent Partner resonate with you?

10. When the unexpected appears, what is your gut reaction?

11. At what point will you seek advice from your Silent Partner?

12. When you come to the bend in the road, how do you react?

Additional Resources

Collins, Jim. *Good to Great: Why Some Companies Make the Leap . . . and Others Don't* (New York: Harper Business, 2001).

Keith, K. M. *Anyway: The Paradoxical Commandments* (New York: G. P. Putnam's Sons, 2001).

Maxwell, John C. *Falling Forward: Turning Mistakes Into Stepping Stones* (Nashville: Thomas Nelson, 2000).

Novak, Michael. *Business as a Calling: Work and the Examined Life* (New York: Free Press, a division of Simon and Shuster, 1996).

Pollard, C. William. *The Soul of the Firm* (Grand Rapids: Zondervan, 1996).

7

Exercising Your Options Is a Healthy Workout

Have I not commanded you? Be strong and courageous.
Do not be terrified; do not be discouraged, for the LORD
your God will be with you wherever you go.

—Joshua 1:9

Now fear the LORD and serve him with all faithfulness . . .
But if serving the LORD seems undesirable to you, then
choose for yourselves this day whom you will serve . . . But as
for me and my household, we will serve the LORD.

—Joshua 24:14–15

I hate to admit it, but I've not always chosen the best options available to me. Those options have ranged from business expansion and opportunities for employment, to serving on boards and building a house—and the list could go on. However, I have tried to make the best of whatever option I chose at the time.

No doubt, money has been left on the table in some of those options. As Jerry's boss (and one of the nation's wealthiest men), Bob Van Kampen often reminded him, "We exercise the right of the second decision." That is, if your first decision seems incorrect, make another one. Don't tarry. Make two or three decisions if necessary. You can always decide to change instead of staying with a decision that is not profitable and doesn't appear to have promise. And oftentimes that means cutting losses and moving on. In Bob's opinion, the sooner the better.

I can say, however, the Lord knew exactly how much I should put on the table, and more specifically, on my plate. He knew what would allow me to sleep comfortably, and in my long business life I've followed this sleep principle: Never make choices that keep you

"Never make choices that keep you from a sound sleep."

from a sound sleep. I have no regrets about my management life. Opportunities missed? Perhaps. Sleepless nights as a result of those decisions? No, because I've prayed and sometimes fasted over major decisions throughout my life. When I left a venture lying on the table, it was because I felt at the time it was the best option for me.

Malcolm in the Marketplace

I recall going into the Guernsey Savings and Loan in Cambridge, Ohio, to obtain a construction loan for a nursing home facility. My business partner and I presented the case for our loan to that institution's president. When we finished, he said, "If you are looking for an immediate answer, I cannot give it. These matters must go before our board." He continued, "If my answer today is not what you are looking for, then I suggest you go to another lending institution." He wisely was not going to make a hasty decision, no matter how good our loan application appeared. He delayed, we delayed, and in due time the loan was granted. He wasn't pressured into making such a major decision quickly. Obviously, he had a solid history and many case studies behind him.

On another occasion during the 1970s, we were looking for ways to expand our business. We needed money desperately to build and operate our facilities, and it was during the time of rampant inflation and very high interest rates. Combining the two, inflation and interest, we had a misery index that registered in the twenties. In order to be able to borrow funds we almost had to prove to the bankers that we really didn't need them.

You're likely laughing, but it wasn't funny at the time. I'm reminded of the early days of Andrew Carnegie's career in which he had the opportunity to invest in his first stock (ten shares of Adams Express stock at $50 per share), and then a chance to invest in what became the Pullman Sleeping Cars. Though he was climbing the corporate ladder and deemed a brilliant mind, he still had to mortgage his family's house.[1]

During our management team's daily prayers we raised this funding need for new facilities and maintaining current operations to the Lord. These prayers were answered in the form of a banker who was interested in getting into our line of business. He had the money and the location for the operation, but had no one with the expertise to build it for him. We received the loan and simultaneously assisted him in getting his building. It proved to be a win-win situation for all of us. Could we have pulled that one off without the Lord as our Senior Partner? Looking back at it, I really don't think so. There were numerous banks and officers, and the chances of meeting him exactly at our mutual times of need were slim without God's intervention.

There are times that the correct option to follow becomes as clear as your nose. In such cases, it takes a lot less contemplation and discussion— although decisions should always include prayer. When the obvious occurs, go with what your experience has taught you—that there is no need for phone calls and board meetings. It's the balance between being too authoritative and earning your wage. We're hired to make decisions even if, in a sense, we've hired ourselves. Our boards will decide on our competencies and habits and on our collective decisions.

Most serious decisions aren't quite as obvious, and we need to take time to consider all our options. Write them down. List the pros and cons of each one along with the facts concerning the pending decision. Once that is completed, sleep on it unless it's an urgent decision. Pray over your list of options. God is true to his Word and he will give you wisdom on which option will be best.

Weighing Service Opportunities

It appears that with management or financial success comes unlimited opportunities to serve. For the most part, the needs of certain ministries or organizations will resonate with us. This can help narrow the list. Even so, hard decisions need to be made.

In the 1980s, I was asked to serve on the board of directors of a very fine Christian university. Although it would have been a very prestigious opportunity, I declined on the basis that I was already serving on another university's board, as well as the board of a seminary. There is only so much time that one can effectively serve in these capacities, especially if you have employment duties to honor.

A little while later, I was presented with an opportunity to serve on a mission board of directors. Since it was for a small Christian organization, I felt that it would not require as much time as the university board, and after prayer and guidance, I accepted.

The chairman of the mission board was one of the owners of the Blue Bird Bus Company. We struck up a great friendship. We began looking for property in the Southeastern United States where we could build a nursing home and retirement center for the mission board. Utilizing our combined resources and a large monetary gift from his family, the venture became a success.

My company managed that operation for a number of years and produced several thousand dollars annually for the mission organization. Though my company is no longer involved in the daily operations of those facilities, they still produce hundreds of thousands of dollars annually for the related ministries.

Don't get in a hurry to make major decisions. If time is indeed money, then it's a good investment to buy yourself some time. Make the decision based on the facts at hand. If new information arises then tweak the decision based on these new facts, assuming time is in your favor. Once the decision is made, and you have chosen your option, then stay with it.

Remember, you have bathed it in prayer and are now looking for your Senior Partner to do all that he can do.

"Don't get in a hurry to make major decisions. If time is indeed money, then it's a good investment to buy yourself some time."

What about bad decisions that have been made? Let those be a guide to you so that you don't repeat them in the future. Learn from your mistakes. Consider the bumps in your business life as stepping stones to a new era. Can we correct our mistakes? In a literal sense, no. But we can correct the results of bad decisions. The prognosis depends on the seriousness of the wrong option exercised. You'll want to rectify the situation if possible. Otherwise, you'll reflect on a second missed opportunity in your years ahead. On many occasions I've not been able to correct errors, but turned them over to the Lord and asked for divine wisdom regarding how to proceed. Some losses are beyond our control, and we made the best decisions given the information we had at the time. I find tremendous comfort in Joel 2:25: God "will repay you for the years the locusts have eaten." This gives assurance that our losses and calamity may get corrected at some later date. We must rely on the Lord.

When We Act without Considering All the Options

One of the more unfortunate situations in business is having uninformed managers. Either they haven't kept current on business trends or marketing projects or they simply aren't observant in the face of choices that take common sense. It may not be book-learning options, but simple life-experience learning. Sometimes knowing a particular commodity index, personnel regulation, or tax law is required. Other times it's making a timely phone call or a second reference check when something sounds suspicious. Common sense can save a lot of cents.

The following story illustrates the absence of both types of learning. It's a true story about travelers who chose the wrong option and had no way to correct it, even though they tried.

Five corpses were discovered alongside the mutilated body of a camel in the Sahara Desert. When the search and rescue team began to put together the pieces of events that preceded this tragedy, they scratched their heads in disbelief. They realized the deceased men had been traveling in a motor vehicle across the desert in a place where there were only markers, not roads. When their vehicle broke down they ignored the rule of the desert to stay with your vehicle. When that rule is followed, if travelers don't arrive at their destinations at appointed times, a search party forms and the missing people are easily found.

These men had options and they chose the wrong one. They disobeyed the conventional wisdom of those experienced in such crises. They wandered away from their vehicle, apparently in pursuit of a camel they saw in the distance. They hurriedly drew closer to the beast as it plodded its way across the sand. As they continued, the sizzling heat became too much for them. They probably reasoned that in the cool of the evening the camel would stop to rest, and then they could tap its water supply.

Not only did they lack conventional wisdom, but knowledge about the camel's anatomy. They figured that somewhere in the camel's hump there must be a pouch, or bladder, that carries excess water.

Eventually, when the camel stopped they killed it, only to be frustrated with the lack of any drinkable water. One rescuer noted, "If only they had continued to follow the camel, they would have found water. The camel would have led them to water. They killed their only hope of survival."

We seem to do this at times in our business lives. In my opinion, our only hope of survival in the management world is our contact with our Senior Partner. In him, we have an immeasurable source of supplies to assist us in our times of need. We should ensure that our communication lines with him are always working.

Whatever the decision, whether managerial or personal, always begin with the Book. Daily reading of God's Word is essential. Certain words and passages will become navigational points. These words are there for us to apply to our present circumstances and decision making. This is promised in Psalm 32:8: "I will instruct you and teach you in the way you should go; I will counsel you and watch over you."

We need to keep this in mind with new ventures as well as current investments and commitments. Even when decisions are made in accordance with the Book, we still face the challenges of new variables. Not all sailing is smooth. I can say that after seventy years I know he takes care of the rough places and gives a peace "that passes all understanding." He's in the boat with us as we navigate life's major decisions.

Learning to Pass the Leadership Torch with God's Blessing

Moses was leading the Israelites towards the Promised Land of Canaan, which roughly corresponds with modern Israel, and he had tough managerial decisions to make. Prior to crossing into Canaan, he chose one leader from each tribe to scout out the land and return with their assessment (Num. 13:1–3 paraphrased).

Only two of them returned with positive reports: Joshua and Caleb. They knew that they could conquer the land and its people. The others offered contrary advice. They told the people that the land was full of warriors and the people were giants. They felt like grasshoppers. And in the light of these reports, Moses and the Israelites didn't go. Instead, they wandered around for forty years before the opportunity presented itself again. This time to the next generation, and those like Joshua who had trusted God.

At the end of Deuteronomy, we find that Moses is aware his life is nearing its end. He commissions Joshua and announces him his successor, chosen by his Senior Partner (Deut. 3:26–29). After Moses' burial on Mt. Nebo, the Israelites were faced with a decision once again: to cross the Jordan River and claim the Promised Land, or disobey God and walk away.

In our businesses, we need assurance that our likely successors think critically, and with a long view. That is, when they recognize the options before them, the easier path might prove to be counterproductive in the light of long-term results. Although the Israelites weren't his employees, they were looking to Joshua for leadership. He was decisive. "Go through the camp and tell the people, 'Get your supplies ready. Three days from now you will cross the Jordan here to go in and take possession of the land the LORD your God is giving you for your own.'" (Josh. 1:11). The people accepted his leadership. "Then they answered Joshua, 'Whatever you have commanded us we will do, and wherever you send us we will go'" (Josh. 1:16).

Oftentimes, like in Joshua's situation, it is important to recall similar crossroads in an organization's past. What options were explored and what were the consequences of the choices made? In the case of Joshua and the Israelites, what changed from forty years earlier? The challenge was similar four decades before: Move forward in faith or stay and face dire consequences. They had learned, but still had no idea of the miracles they were about to witness. Their parents had seen God send plagues and part the Red Sea. And, along with their families, they had seen the daily miracle of manna. They knew of God's power, but still not exhaustively. In just a few short days the walls of Jericho would fall, and they would experience firsthand what they already knew in principle. That is, God has power over the things of this world.

God's assistance is available for us too. He controls markets and the marketplace. While rarely do our businesses face the life or death consequences that the Israelites faced, we do face the consequences of being led by God.

As a young manager, I was given the task of supervising a truck fleet that was operating throughout the Midwest. Burly truck drivers don't take very kindly towards young managers. I heard it all, including remarks such as, "What do you know—you're still wet behind the ears?"

This particular fleet of about forty units had a rather poor safety record, and I was supposed to address it. Some of the drivers had died in traffic fatalities.

After about a year on the job, one of my drivers called me at midnight. He had been traveling with three other drivers from Chicago to our base in Ohio. He suddenly came upon a wreck on the highway. Two trucks had collided and both were on fire. Both drivers were dead—one was ours. Suddenly, and under sad circumstances, the word safety took on a whole new meaning.

After being raked over the coals by the Interstate Commerce Commission, I was charged with enacting a whole new set of safety regulations for our fleet. Strict attention to drivers' hours, rest periods, and speeds were the order of the day. The task was complicated by the attitude of earthy, veteran drivers claiming to know how to survive on the road.

I found myself with my back against the wall on more than one occasion, trying to reason with our drivers about the necessity of our new rules and regulations. It would have been easier for me to find employment elsewhere—to cut and run. I was facing some giants, literally and figuratively. However, after a three-year period under the new safety plan, our fleet earned the prestigious Trailmobile Fleet Safety Award for being the best type of operation in our class in the state of Ohio.

Was it easy? Certainly not! Was it worthwhile? Yes! And there are drivers who lived to work another day as a result of the rules that were put in place.

More Lessons from Joshua

Joshua called a meeting of his followers shortly before his death. He reminded them of all of God's blessings. To paraphrase, "God gave you land that you had not worked for; he gave you cities that you did not build;

he gave you vineyards and olive groves for food that you did not plant; so revere God and serve him in sincerity and truth" (see Josh. 24:13–14).

My hope is that, like those listening to Joshua, you've come to realize that God has your best interests in mind, and you should put God first in your life. Thank him for all you have received from his hand. I believe that the peace that comes from this, and the guidance you receive through prayer and his Word, will help you to be a better leader.

Joshua implored his people to "choose for yourselves this day whom you will serve," He went on to say, "as for me and my household, we will serve the LORD" (Josh. 24:15).

You will constantly be faced with options. Some options that will make your business profitable, and others that, though promising on the surface, will actually cost you money. You will constantly be faced with honest and honorable routes to your goals and, simultaneously, with unethical pursuits. Serve the Lord with all your heart and reap those benefits. Otherwise you'll reap ephemeral gains. Joshua challenges us to choose whom we will serve. Make the right choice.

When Fatigue Wears You Out

During the mid-1980s I was suffering seriously from business fatigue. My energy would depart unannounced any time during the day. Some days fatigue would strike at 9:00 a.m. after what promised to be a great morning. Other times it happened during evening business deals. I self-diagnosed my problem as some sort of a serious physical ailment, though a recent annual physical had revealed nothing unusual. Within two months, I returned to the hospital and requested that the physicians redo my physical. It had to be some type of serious blood condition, or so I thought.

After a solid battery of tests, they once again cleared me of any serious illness, but gave me a diagnosis I wasn't expecting: "Malcolm, your problem is simple—you're suffering from fatigue." I wasn't even sure what that meant, but I soon learned that the only cure, and one I had to abide by, was to take some measurable time off work.

When I presented this situation to my business partner, with signed papers from my physician, we agreed that I should go to half time for an undetermined period. We devised a plan whereby I could work about part time until this fatigue had passed. Well, what sounded like a great answer actually took about six months to implement. Even then, I continued working about three-fourths time and finally realized the best way to reach my hoped-for prognosis was to leave the organization. It came down to this: What are my best options?

When facing fatigue, we need to determine the difference between a temporary commitment to an intense overload and normal expectations. Perhaps it sounds elementary, but we need to mark our calendars, whether the traditional wall calendar next to our fridge or a fancier Microsoft Project Gant chart, to an intense overload and a standing expectation. Signify the end of a start-up or ramp-up period. Inform your spouse of your planned workload, and pray through this. If that time comes, and you can't keep your promise to self and spouse to limit overtime, ask the types of questions related to my options above. For example, "Are there recurring duties that are linked to my repetitive overloads?" And, "Is there evidence that I'm controlling my schedule, or does it appear that the schedule is controlling me?"

My writing partner once found himself logging two hundred thousand bonus miles in ten months, as a result of traveling to offices in Hereford, England; Grand Haven, Michigan; and Wadi Natrun, Egypt. At the end of a two-year commitment, he chose to walk away from this dream job—because it was someone else's dream. Jerry unpacks this in his book, *Why I Teach: And Why It Matters to My Students*. He told me that in his late thirties, he found himself saying to his wife, "If I don't get out of this, I'll be dead by fifty." Well, that likely would have been my scenario as well. I'm now in my seventies and Jerry just turned fifty, and I am confident that God helped us to make the right choices.

A great reference for dealing with the busyness of business is Mark 6:31. During a hectic time when crowds of people kept the apostles so busy that they missed lunch, Jesus said to them, "Come with me by yourselves to a quiet place and get some rest" (Mark 6:31). I find here four key aspects of regaining strength.

First, find a quiet place. It could be an office with a closed door, a hotel, a beach, or a café, but it needs to be away from the busyness that is wearing on you.

Second, "rest a while" (Mark 6:31 KJV), or as it says in another translation, "get some rest" (Mark 6:31). We need to be careful not to think of always needing extended periods of time off. In fact, the Sabbath is a good example of a weekly short respite amidst busyness.

Third, either be alone or gather with like-minded people. As you'll see a bit later, our company considered a designated prayer time with our staff as one such occasion for rest and refreshment.

And fourth, take Christ with you. It's one thing to take time off for a much-needed vacation. It's quite another to do so for spiritual replenishment as well.

A year after I attempted to implement a fatigue plan, I found myself, after much prayer and some fasting, bidding farewell to my business partner. I decided the best recourse was to go in a different direction. Two of my sons had been working for the same organization, and they encouraged me to get into a similar business and take them along as partners, which we did. However, starting up a new business had its new share of challenges and responsibilities. This time I entered with a fatigue prevention plan—special group prayer sessions at work.

My Senior Partner helped us miraculously to acquire five businesses within a one-year period. Could I have done that without God's assistance? I think not. It took us nearly five years to acquire the next business. We were doing well with five such businesses that I believe God helped us to acquire the amount necessary for financial success. The icing on the cake came when he supplied us with the sixth such business venture. Also, the Lord knew we needed all those operations to become reasonably successful.

A tremendous amount of prayer went into the operation of those businesses. Every Monday morning we gathered with all our staff in the home office for prayer before beginning any work for that day and week. In addition to normal staffing and business needs, for many months we prayed for as many as ten new employees. Common among the requests were safety for travel, and unlike the modern sitcom, *The Office,* in which actor Steve Carell is constantly calling meetings to scheme of ways to outdo other branches, our various locations grew close through these prayer times.

Our Senior Partner honored our time spent before him. In retrospect, and with the benefit of notes from those prayer times, we did not have one serious need that was not met in his timing. And, fatigue subsided. As you read this book about management principles, I'd be remiss not to emphasize the value of these prayer times. Reflection often informs actions and focuses reactions—a habit of prayer among peers is proactive.

We operated those businesses successfully for a ten-year period, and then we were faced with another option: Continue operating as we had been doing, or accept an offer from a large company aggressively seeking to purchase businesses such as ours. I had often joked with my wife and some of our business partners that if a sizeable offer ever came our way, then we should take the money and run. What was meant as a joke, however, became an option we could not have imagined early in our business. A decision to sell some businesses in which we were minority shareholders brought financial freedom that still has a positive impact on what my wife and I can do to further God's kingdom—and do so at no cost to the ministries we help.

My new friends, please take this valuable lesson from my business journey without exception, exercise your options only after consulting with the Senior Partner. You may not understand the impact of those options for quite some time, perhaps for a decade or more, but God is faithful and will give you a peace that passes all understanding.

A Lesson on Options from My Military Travels

My cousin, retired colonel Robert (Bob) E. Vickers, was honored in Cambridge, England, at the American Air Museum of Duxford in 2002. My wife and I were privileged to attend. Colonel Vickers is a member of the board of directors for the museum and served thirty-three years in the Air Force. Bob had been the pilot of a B-24 Liberator Bomber and flew thirty missions. A restored B-24 was present at the ceremony, and it had all the markings of his plane, the *Dugan*. He was joined by three members of his crew, former President George H. W. Bush, and Prince Charles of England.

All the missions that Bob and his crew members had flown had been successful except one. In January of 1945, the crew had started a bombing run over an oil refinery in Germany. As they approached the target, one of the four engines flak struck and had to be turned off immediately since it was spewing oil. Flak is a shell filled with metal that is timed to explode at a given altitude. No sooner had the crew reported one engine out, when another engine on the other side of the plane began spewing oil. That engine had to be turned off as well.

With two engines out, the crew knew there was no hope of trying to keep up with the rest of the invasion force on their return trip to their base in England. A quick decision had to be made. No time for drills. No time to be reading manuals. No time to call the home office and ask for help. They considered their options:

Option 1: Ride the plane as far as they could until enemy fighters showed up.

Option 2: Parachute immediately and become prisoners of war, if they were successful in getting to the ground alive.

Option 3: Hope the plane would hold up long enough to get out of enemy territory and reach a landing in friendly territory.

They began to pray. They chose Option 3. Suddenly, the crew looked up and saw two American fighter planes. They broke radio silence and asked for help. The reply: "We will escort you as far as our fuel will allow. We will then point you in the direction of friendly territory."

A few minutes later, the crippled plane had to fly over Frankfurt, Germany. Because they had broken radio silence, a Germany artillery post was waiting for them. The post opened fire and destroyed the third of the four engines. The plane began to lose altitude and the crew knew it was only a matter of time before it would crash. They began throwing out all the loose equipment that they could in order to lighten the load and hopefully land a little closer to friendly territory.

Fortunately for the crew, the navigator had done his homework before the flight began and knew approximately where the enemy lines met up with friendly lines. He had studied the *Stars and Stripes* newspaper early that morning and knew how far allied troops had advanced. He suddenly saw a river ahead and determined they were about to enter allied territory.

The plane continued to descend, even with full power operating on the one remaining engine. They bailed out as the plane began to wobble, but not before they crossed the river. All crew members landed safely in allied territory. They were taken into the houses of friendly French civilians and were later reunited with their American comrades.

There often comes a time in decision making when you have only one option left. Do lots of praying, as the plane crew did, and hope for the best. When we have done all that we can do, then our Senior Partner will do all that he can do.

Questions for Reflection

1. Have you faced a choice and chosen to run from it? If so, did you find yourself needing to face it at a later date?

2. In the case of the Hebrew spies, they saw giants and lost their belief in God's power. When is the last time you've faced a giant, and how did you respond?

3. If you're a risk taker, how well do you sleep at night?

4. When the going gets tough, how to you react?

5. How do you make decisions?

6. How certain are you about God's place in your future?

7. Think about a time in which you chose the wrong option. What did you attempt in order to correct it?

8. By listing the various options that can be used when making important decisions, how do you go about doing them?

9. There are many worthwhile non-profit entities that need your expertise. How will you go about getting involved in one or two?

10. What process do you use to make sure that your decisions are being made in accordance with God's will for your life?

11. What is your strategy for facing severe obstacles?

Additional Resources

Beckett, J. D. *Loving Monday: Succeeding in Business without Selling Your Soul* (Downers Grove, Ill.: InterVarsity Press, 1998).

Maxwell, John C. *The 21 Irrefutable Laws of Leadership: Follow Them and People Will Follow You* (Nashville: Thomas Nelson, 1999).

Millage, P. *Created for Accomplishment* (Fishers, Ind.: Marketing Solutions, Inc., 2006).

Nash, Laura. *Believers in Business* (Nashville: Thomas Nelson, 1994).

Peters, Thomas J. and Robert H. Waterman, Jr. *In Search of Excellence: Lessons from America's Best-Run Companies* (New York: Warner Books, 1982).

8

Wise Advice Is
to Seek It

*Pride only breeds quarrels, but wisdom
is found in those who take advice.*

−Proverbs 13:10

Oftentimes we think of prominent business leaders as having all the answers, but that's rarely the case. Usually you'll find that they surround themselves with good staff, or as we see in the early days of J. Paul Getty's success, the willingness to ask for help.

In the oil business, and first noted in a 1957 *Fortune* magazine article, J. Paul Getty had become the wealthiest man in the world.[1] Early in his career, he owned a seventy-two-square-foot piece of property in the middle of the Seal Beach oil field in California. Unfortunately, oil derricks were much too large to fit on his property.

While people were laughing at Getty and calling his little piece of real estate "Getty's Turnip Patch," Getty was meeting with his drilling crews and asking them for help to solve the problem. Before long, his employees came up with the idea of building a miniature oil derrick to fit on the miniature piece of ground.

But they had one more problem. To get to the property all they had was a four-foot right-of-way. So they went to work and built a miniature railroad track to carry their miniature derrick to their seventy-two-square-foot plot of ground. Before long they had drilled a well that began producing thousands of barrels of oil each year. The creative ideas of a highly praised work crew paid off handsomely for Getty. People need to be needed. Getty very wisely tapped into those needs and it became a win-win situation for both him and his employees.

Malcolm in the Marketplace

As a kid growing up in Ohio in the 1940s, I was always on the lookout to make a buck. Well, it was more like five or ten cents in those days.

One of my ventures was to sell packets of seeds in the spring and Cloverine Salve in the off season. My strategy for selling was simple. I would knock on the prospect's door and prepare my sales pitch while waiting for someone to answer. That was the extent of my long-term marketing strategy.

My best marketing technique was then put into play as I firmly stated, "You don't want to buy any seeds (or salve) do you?" Well, many of my clients took pity on me and bought in spite of my faults. This all changed when a gracious gentleman took me aside and encouraged me to change my sales pitch to something a little more positive.

"I am selling seeds (or salve). How many would you like to buy?" Although I wasn't searching for advice regarding a more effective game plan at the time, his words proved extremely valuable.

When the stakes were much higher later in life, I often sought advice. When the headquarters of our business relocated from Minnesota to Indiana, I wanted to know how we could become more successful in our line of work. I sought out the operators of similar businesses whom I had learned were very successful, and promptly went to them for help. Their names were Wally Miller and Don Norman. They were experts in the field of health care and were at the top of the business in Indiana. They invited me to sit at their feet and be mentored, for which I am still grateful. I learned a great deal from them that in turn saved our company a lot of money.

My advice to you is to seek all the advice you can when starting a business of your own or while you are working for someone else in a managerial role. Successful people are usually very warm and cordial when telling others about how they attained their personal success. This matches the profile of Level Five Leaders.

Another area where a manager can acquire some sound advice is through attending seminars that relate to one's particular operation, and the Wharton School of Business at the University of Pennsylvania is a good place to start. Summer seminars and certificate programs have a variety of fee structures, but the insight gained will be worth much more than the cost of admission (www.wharton.upenn.edu). It only takes one transferable idea, whether a policy or practice, to make the investment pay off. If the price of admission seems high, and you're trying to find free advice, then keep in mind that you usually get what you pay for.

Solomon is widely regarded as one of the wisest men the world has ever known. We find much of his excellent advice throughout the book of Proverbs. Yet, how many of us refuse to accept good advice when it is offered. Why do we refuse it? Is it because we think we have a better way to do things? Perhaps. Or maybe our pride prohibits us from asking. This attitude will put you in an extremely precarious position in this hi-tech age. One of the leading experts in dealing with this younger generation of digital natives is Marc Prensky.[2] He notes that one of our biggest mistakes is not asking our children and students to teach us. Instead, we'll go to a half-day workshop to learn something they could show us in minutes.

Your Employees Need to Be Needed

The most valuable resource that any employer has is its people, and they need to feel needed. We live in transient work times, and employees will move to another employer for a better work environment if it demonstrates they are needed. Treat the people who work for you like family.

Seek advice from your employees; ask for their opinions. People seem to be rejuvenated when they realize their opinions are appreciated. Advice givers will begin to open up. Once again, remember the Golden Rule: Do to others what you would have them do to you. In other words, treat others the way you want to be treated.

Management is meeting the needs of people as they work at accomplishing their jobs. It's perhaps counterintuitive, but the successful leader practices service, or what leadership programs are calling service leadership. In a sense, this whole concept is the outworking of the Golden Rule. This service approach will also help to lessen the incidence of sexual harassment, job discrimination, and the like. These issues often occur when managers focus on themselves instead of others.

Several years ago, I was serving our country as a soldier in the army. I had been assigned to Fort Knox, Kentucky, in order to get my training for the next assignment. The schooling and training had ended, and I was headed to Fort Bliss, Texas.

Upon arrival at Fort Bliss, I found myself being interviewed for a position at post headquarters. Two of my traveling companions were being interviewed for the same job. I was the last to be interviewed. I felt certain that they would select one of the others over me because they possessed some qualifications that I did not have.

To my surprise, they offered me the position. When I asked why, the deciding officer said "Those two men are single. They will be asking to transfer out of here to Germany because that is where all the action is for a single man. Since you are married, I want to ask you a question: If I give you this position, would you like to invite your wife to come and live here on the base with you?" That was like asking me if I were to receive a million dollars as a gift, would I promise to spend it?

The officer did not realize that my wife and I had been praying that I would get stationed somewhere in the States so that she could join me. When I answered in the positive, the officer said, "Oh, and one more thing. I am going to allow you to borrow leave time to go home and pick up your wife and bring her here. Is that okay with you?" This officer was a people manager; he was genuinely interested in others.

I stayed on at the Fort Bliss, Texas post for the remaining time in the military and worked for that particular officer until my discharge after the mandatory two-year period. I have always been grateful to Major George Webber for extending to me his genuine interest in my personal welfare while I was under his command.

We have all met people who are genuinely interested in others, people who will make time for us and voluntarily assist us in making decisions. They give advice even when we do not ask for it at the time, but it's exactly what we need.

Most of the time, it is more fun giving advice than taking it. After all, if someone has to give us advice, it is usually because we have strayed off course and they are attempting to bring us back. Whatever the reason, we normally just want to shrug it off and go on about our business.

A number of years ago while teaching a series of workshops to business leaders in former Communist countries, some leaders of marketing firms, speaker bureaus, and various companies and I were trying to bring about a paradigm shift. In one instance, we were attempting to get the class to explore new ideas about business management. The attendees, regional business leaders, had become accustomed to having others make the key decisions while they merely completed work assignments. In a sense, some higher authority would always do the thinking for them. How could we get them to change their way of thinking and begin to make managers of them?

We used a simple object lesson using nine dots on a blackboard. The dots were placed in three rows with three dots in each row. They were spaced about one foot apart.

The class participants were asked to come forward and connect all the dots by using only one continuous line and not lifting the chalk off the blackboard at any time. Rarely could anyone complete the exercise as planned.

Most people, in attempting this exercise, attempt to connect all the dots within the box of nine dots. They could not think beyond the area in which the dots were located.

We would then reveal the answer, using one continuous line by going outside the box of nine dots. In this manner, we were teaching them how to think beyond the box and to expand their acceptance of new ideas. Remember, a mind stretched to a new idea never returns to its original dimension.

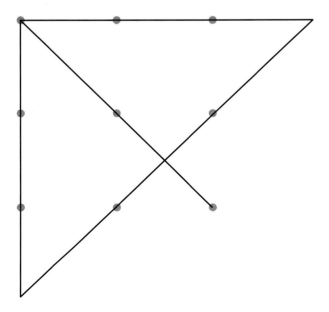

Giving Advice

When you are presented with questions that, in your view, have obvious solutions, don't take them lightly—they likely have important answers. Allow me to explain. As mentioned above, many people from Eastern Europe (the former Communist countries) were not allowed to think for themselves in the past. A few years ago, I remember discussing the use of the *Jesus* film with a particular Eastern European Christian denomination. Many good people from the U.S. were traveling in those countries and showing the film wherever they could muster an audience. However, this particular church denomination was taking offense at the film's conclusion, after the dramatization of the Jesus story.

There was an appeal in the end of the film for viewers seeking additional information about Christianity, and it encouraged them to contact a local Catholic priest. Since that statement proved problematic to the sponsoring denomination, they wanted permission to do something about it. However, the solution was there all along and easily within their purview. When asked for advice, I encouraged them simply to turn off the film. They could complete the service with their own announcement. Their response: "Would we be allowed to do that?"

They still were looking for permission from a higher power for any change. They didn't realize that their new freedom would allow them to do whatever they pleased. Although I thought they were asking for advice on a no-brainer, it was a very serious matter to them. I had to remind myself of their past experience in order to understand their uneasiness.

If you're successful, people should be asking your advice. It's not always clear why people seek me out: My gray hair? My age? Perhaps they may have some knowledge of my career. While these times may be somewhat flattering, the important thing is that I may help others to avoid some pitfalls. Simultaneously, it's an affirmation of my own work and a challenge to continue a healthy profile. I also use these times to build in accountability, asking the advice seekers to give me periodic updates.

I recall a man whose wife was in the women's fitness business. He asked me for advice. They were operating in a large building and her clientele was growing. Everything seemed positive, but they were still losing money.

I gave them the usual advice, such as how to make a budget, resources for free advertising advice, and how to structure a business plan. We discovered the greatest strategic need was for additional clients, and after a couple hours of discussion, the husband's mistaken notion was that the most pressing need was for a new computer.

However, he should have sought his wife's advice, not just mine. He was attempting to operate the business without full input from his wife— his business partner. Although she had a much better feel for operations, he didn't seek her advice. Needless to say, the venture failed and the couple moved away. They did not pursue any similar ventures again. This is similar to the Anderson Window ad, "Only the rich can afford poor windows."

Sometimes our advice fails for lack of proper implementation. Solomon confirms that "wisdom is found in those who take advice" (Prov. 13:10). He encourages us to seek good advice.

Leaders Recognize Solid Advice

While teaching Ethics in Business in Eastern Europe during the mid-1990s, my topic on a particular day was "Ten Principles of Ethical Decision Making" based on the Ten Commandments. During the lesson, I was careful not to make it sound like a ten-point sermon. This presentation was made just prior to our breaking for lunch in the same building.

Since this building housed an active factory, we were given tours of the operations as soon as lunch was over. Each day of the three-day seminar, we were given a tour of a different aspect of their production. The plant manager instituted a program of having all our cameras picked up and stored away while we were at lunch and touring the facility. The man in charge of taking our cameras was, unknown to us, also the head of the plant union. I was about to find out that fact for myself.

While giving my lecture, some segments seemed to resonate with the audience. At one point I was giving advice on how to treat others and made a reference to my father's drinking problem. I noticed during the translation from English that some of the women began to weep. I didn't know all that was transpiring, only hoping that no one's feelings were hurt. I discovered later that many of them were being abused by their alcoholic husbands.

The talk ended, we gathered our cameras, turned them in, and we were off to lunch—or so I thought. When the gentleman took my camera, the translator said, "He wants to see you right away in his office." I didn't know why, but surmised that something in my talk had proved offensive.

I immediately asked a colleague to join me. Once we were inside his office he instructed us to sit. He then pulled out a pocket-size, antiquated tape recorder. He proceeded to state that he had recorded everything that I had said, making me rather uneasy.

As he was talking I recognized the Solidarity symbol on his wall. I then knew this man represented the union for the entire plant, making me even more uneasy since our talks resonated more with business than union personnel. But I was mistaken. He shocked me by saying, "I am going to take this recording home to my family and let them hear it because I believe everything you said in the seminar. I am also going to teach it to all the two thousand employees in this factory. This is something that everyone should hear."

I thanked him for his kind words and left the room with my colleague. In the cafeteria I said to my friend, "Don't ever tell me there is no God." My fears had been unfounded, and I silently thanked the Lord for taking care of me in what I thought could have been an unfortunate incident.

The camera man, or union man, whichever you choose to call him, was a true leader. He demonstrated this to me that day in Elk, Poland. Leaders understand that people need people. People form relationships because they have needs that can only be met by other people. Unmet needs erode relationships. I found a friend that day who believed that Biblical principles had the potential of transforming lives.

Apply the truths found in the Book. You will become wise and your counsel will be sought by other people.

Questions for Reflection

1. How difficult is it for you to seek advice?

2. What part of your management focus should be to meet the needs of your employees?

3. "Only the rich can afford poor windows." What does this mean to you?

4. How do you handle criticism?

5. Where do you turn to seek wisdom?

6. What is the best advice you've received? What did you do with it?

Additional Resources

Kroeker, Wally. *God's Week Has 7 Days: Monday Musings for Marketplace Christians* (Waterloo, Ontario, Canada: Herald Press, 1998).

Mahedy, The Rev. William and Dr. Christopher Carstens. *Starting on Monday: Christian Living in the Workplace* (New York: Ballentine / Epiphany, Ballentine Books, 1987).

Maxwell, John C. *The Difference Maker: Making Your Attitude Your Greatest Asset* (Nashville: Thomas Nelson, 2006).

_____. *The 360 Degree Leader: Developing Your Influence from Anywhere in the Organization* (Nashville: Thomas Nelson, 2006).

9

Givers and Takers

Give, and it will be given to you. A good measure, pressed down,
shaken together and running over, will be poured into your lap.
For with the measure you use, it will be measured to you.

–Luke 6:38

If your business ventures become successful, then you'll have good problems on your hands—how much to give away and where to give it. John Wesley said, "Make all you can. Save all you can. Give all you can." Many people are in business because they have sensed God's call to do so. For some, it's a career that aligns directly with their birthright strengths. In many ways these gifts allow you to lead both at work and in your church and community—and oftentimes through financial support.

The Bible gives us some straightforward advice on this account. "'Bring the whole tithe into the storehouse, that there may be food in my house. Test me in this,' says the LORD Almighty, 'and see if I will not throw open the floodgates of heaven and pour out so much blessing that you will not have room enough for it'" (Mal. 3:10). The purpose of tithing—giving one-tenth of our income—is to teach us always to put God first in our lives (see Deut. 14:23).

My hope is that your desire to give inspires you to earn. Giving to the Lord is both a duty and privilege; it's an honor. As I'm nearing the end of my business career, I'm much more focused on giving. My wife and I have attempted to be intentional in where and why we give, and to be open to special needs as they arise. The only reason I would have enjoyed earning more money during my career is to enhance our giving capacity during our retirement years.

Malcolm in the Marketplace

I always enjoyed spending time with Joe Luce, former co-owner of the Blue Bird Bus Company. We first met on a trip to England on a mission trip. We traveled to Germany to join a company that was constructing a large hydro-electric generator for a mission project we both represented. We often traveled together to Honduras to support and remain current on a farm school for young Honduran boys. The boys were taught trades in wood- and metalworking, as well as agriculture and livestock. We eventually collaborated in constructing a nursing home and retirement center for that same missions board.

Every excursion with Joe was a learning experience. His obsession with missions support was inspiring and contagious. Joe was a giver. If a mission field needed something, whether a tractor or a piece of heavy earthmoving equipment, Joe found a way to deliver it. Following his wonderful example, none of our ventures ever cost the mission organizations a dime.

Joe Luce's goal was to time his giving to die broke. His life was a vivid picture of the radical views espoused by Andrew Carnegie: "The man who dies thus rich dies disgraced."[1] Joe's life spoke volumes to me. He left a legacy of giving. Numerous projects and missionaries are thriving today because of his obedience to God with his finances. He expended the same focus and intensity in his benevolence as he did in running his businesses. He's missed, but yet his character and compassion live on. My prayer is that many others will catch his vision. His life mantra was that you cannot out-give God, and this view has found a significant place in my marriage.

Dealing with Educational Requests

All of my business colleagues are regularly approached by a wide range of educational groups worthy of support. Some take the shotgun approach, spreading their donations. I suppose most of us do this to some degree, regardless of our income level. My main interests have been in a local Christian K–12 school where my grandchildren attend and a local Christian college where I have personal roots: Indiana Wesleyan University.

The president of the university came into my office one day and handed me a business card. Not a calling card from him, but a personal request. It simply stated, "Special Assistant to the President of IWU." He went on to say that he was asking me to do some work on behalf of the university and my remuneration would be one dollar. That's right—one dollar per year.

My response was very professional, yet simple. "I will be most happy to do what I can for the school, however, I would prefer not to use a calling card." His next request was somewhat predictable. To make a long story short, he wanted my wife and me to be recognized in the naming of a new two hundred-bed dormitory that was near completion. In the light of our discussion above about having a giving spirit, we considered ourselves fortunate to be able to respond to such a pressing need. Whenever we pass Evans Hall or hear from some of the young women residents, we're reminded of how God has been faithful and how important it is to align our giving with a vibrant ministry.

"An institution is a systematic response to a recurring need. As givers, we consider how our response will help the institution in its ability to respond."

Education by its very nature will always need financial help. By our very nature we'll always have an interest in the welfare of children and our next generation—the future of our country and church. It's when our mission aligns with that of an institution's (and our emotions are touched) that we begin to touch our funds. An institution is a systematic response to a recurring need. As givers, we consider how our response will help the institution in its ability to respond.

While we considered involvement in this project a blessing, we've passed on requests too numerous to recall; we wanted to avoid what Andrew Carnegie labels as counterproductive: "indiscriminate charity."[2] Oftentimes the funds requested were to be used to cover an organization's debt. For example, I've heard requests such as, "Our not-for-profit organization is going to end up several dollars short at the end of our fiscal year." And this is usually followed with, "How much of that would you like to cover?" My answer is always a resounding "None," which usually startles the person.

I then give them this scenario. "When my businesses fail to produce a profit, I have two choices to make. Either I must increase my income or cut my expenses in order to end the year in the black. I suggest you go and do the same." For that same reason, I never have been inclined to underwrite another company's debt. Never give funds in order to cover up poor management practices. Sound ministry practices are also well managed or they're ephemeral regardless of your gift. Strong giving does not remedy weak fiscal management.

A Giver's Focus Should Always Be on Others, not on Self

There are two kinds of people: givers and takers. We are one or the other. We cannot be both. Takers are always looking inward: How can I make things better for me? What can you do for me? What's in it for me? That is their mindset. Givers are constantly looking around to see how they can help someone or some organization. The differences are likely obvious to you.

Andrew Carnegie's description of givers among society's men of wealth is rather straightforward, and applies to any level of financial success. Such a person should strive to:

set an example of modest, unostentatious living, shunning display or extravagance; to provide modestly for the legitimate wants of those dependent upon him [family]; and, after doing so, to consider all surplus revenues which have come to him simply as trust funds, which he is called upon to administer, and strictly bound as a matter of duty to administer in the manner which, in his best judgment, is calculated to produce the most beneficial results for the community—the man of wealth therefore becoming the mere trustee and agent for his poorer brethren, bringing to their service his superior wisdom, experience and ability to administer, doing what they could not or would not do for themselves.[3]

A very simple test is in the most basic area of giving—tithing. The giver will respond positively to God's call for us to "bring the whole tithe into the storehouse." God promises that if we do this, he will "throw open the floodgates of heaven and pour out so much blessing that you will not have room enough for it" (Mal. 3:10). I sometimes think that all my best management practices would have garnered only modest success for my wife, Nadine, and me if they had been void of this principle. I'm convinced that our ability to give today is inextricably linked to our lifetime of tithing and giving at the basic level, not the special projects. The latter comes after the former and both are for God. We give out of obedience to him.

Charity begins at home, and the recipients will take on different faces for each of us. However, in addition to the starting point, tithing, there are other common categories. For most of us, as we look around to see who has needs, there are some rather close to us. Before giving nationally, pay attention to the worthy organizations in your back yard. Similar to our reputation for raising our own children, our testimony will be measured by our engagement with local causes.

As noted above, the learning process is important not only to the future of our country, but also to that of our church. While your focus may be elsewhere, I decided long ago to concentrate my educational giving on church-related enterprises. The Christian K–12 school and the college I support are both associated with my church's denomination. It's not that they're better than those of other denominations, or that their teaching and learning are professionally better than the public school system, but they're attached to my own spiritual history, and they're both local. For many of you, your spiritual journey may be most closely linked with a non-denominational enterprise or parachurch organization; if that is the case then your giving will likely follow.

Specific mission organizations are other areas that we can target our giving. We need to remember that these gifts are not our tithe (though most churches designate part of the tithes for such causes), but these are additional offerings.

There are projects outside of the immediate community that would greatly benefit from extended giving. We could spend our entire waking lives studying requests of worthy organizations. My friends running foundations do just that—they have entire staffs to sort out and manage such requests. The best advice here is, except for token gifts, only reach for your wallet when the cause's mission directly intersects with yours. God gives you such a mission, and he will help you to see such intersections.

Personal Lessons from Dave Dravecky: The Question of Giving or Taking

Many professional athletes have squandered their talent, money, and reputation, whether through dog fighting like Michael Vick, or bizarre strip club shootings like several NBA players. However, baseball pitcher Dave Dravecky still serves as a positive role model. Like the very candid testimony of the 2007 Heisman Trophy winner, Tim Tebow, about his own faith, Dave is rather straightforward about his faith and what it means to his professional and personal life.

Dave was a top major league baseball pitcher who lost his pitching arm to cancer. What a tremendous loss! His means of earning an income was suddenly taken away.

I first met Dave in 1991 when he came to speak at Indiana Wesleyan University for a Marion Christian Business Men's function. This occasion began an enduring friendship with him and his wife, Jan.

When Dave came to speak, it had been only five months since his arm had been amputated. Dave was struggling with the loss of his career as well as anxiety over the possible recurrence of cancer. At that particular point in time, Dave and Jan had no way of knowing what the future had in store for them.

Dave had a great story to tell about a terrific comeback after his initial operation to remove cancerous tumors from the deltoid muscle in his pitching arm. The San Francisco Giants threw a "Welcome Back Dave" celebration that drew fifty thousand Dravecky fans. Everyone wondered whether his arm would hold up. Did he still have the stuff that successful major league pitchers were made of? When the day came for the test—returning to the major leagues and the day of his welcome back party—Dave had a surprisingly strong outing and appeared well on his way to complete recovery. The fans were behind every pitch as Dave chalked up another victory.

A few games later, however, while Dave was pitching, his arm broke—snapped in half before the media and millions of people. Dave tumbled off the mound in a scene that has been replayed countless times. His pitching career was over.

Dave often reflects on that moment when he writhed in pain beside the mound. In his book, *When You Can't Come Back*, Dave states it this way. "Okay, God, what's the next chapter gonna be?" Later on, he states, "The God I serve will take care of me. I don't know how he will do it, but I do know that my faith in him will carry me through."[4]

Dave and Jan have gone on to a successful career in ministering to other cancer patients through their organization, Dravecky's Outreach of Hope. Through their monthly newsletter, *The Encourager*, they provide hope and comfort to thousands of people experiencing similar circumstances. They are expending considerable time encouraging others through their writing and nationwide speaking tours.

Reflecting on the Draveckys' life decisions, I'm reminded again that we share this world with two types of people: givers and takers. Let me ask you as a successful or novice business person: Which are you now, and which will you be at the end of your career? By the time you finish this chapter, you will know which you are.

Givers are those who are always thinking of others in a positive way. They are always answering the question: How may I help you? How can I make your life a little more fulfilling? What can I do for you today? What can I do for you over the coming weeks, months, or even years? In other words, their thoughts are always on someone else and not on themselves. They not only know the Golden Rule, but they practice it daily.

Lessons from Giving and Income Levels

Nadine and I started a program several years ago of trying to out-give God with our finances. Influenced by the lives of people like Dave Dravecky, Joe Luce, and Stanley Tam, we have learned firsthand that the phrase "You can't out-give God" is more than just a catchy quip. It's true.

The program we put into practice is really rather simple. Each year we would increase our giving over and above what we had given the previous year. Of course, the Lord's work would be the beneficiary, through various religious and charitable organizations. The result of that program was, by year's end, we had received additional income which more than offset the increase of our giving. We have been blessed to experience God opening up the windows of heaven and pouring out a blessing on us that we cannot contain. Through the years we can attest to the promises of Luke 6:38 and Deuteronomy 14:23. We establish our faith giving amount each January. In time, our annual giving grew to more than five times what our annual income was the year we started this program!

As I close this chapter on giving, I'm reminded of a trip to London's Westminster Abbey. This historic church contains the remains of many kings, queens, and notable persons. Perhaps the most striking display is the sign over the tomb of the Unknown Warrior: "They buried him among the Kings because he had done good toward God and toward his house."

May similar words be said of you when you lay down for the last time after your life's work. For business men and women, it's how we disburse our personal resources to others (whether privately or publicly) that often establishes our reputation (Prov. 3:27).

Questions for Reflection

1. What motivates you to tithe?

2. What portions of Scripture support the concept of tithing? (As a special challenge, find ALL biblical references to this practice.)

3. When it comes to monetary things, how would your closest friends describe you?

4. In what practical ways can you increase your yearly charitable giving?

5. How will you determine which charitable organizations will receive your donations?

Additional Resources

Mattox, Robert. *The Christian Employee* (Plainfield, N.J.: Logos International, 1978).

Maxwell, John C. *Winning with People: Discover the People Principles that Work for You Every Time* (Nashville: Thomas Nelson, 2006).

Oster, Merrill J. and Mike Hamel. *Giving Back: Using Your Influence to Create Social Change* (Colorado Springs: NavPress, 2003).

10

Plan Your Work then Work Your Plan

*By wisdom a house is built, and through understanding
it is established; through knowledge its rooms are
filled with rare and beautiful treasures.*

−Proverbs 24:3–4

Wise planning begins with an idea, but a good idea is a job only half done. As you're likely aware, many people approach business men and women with great ideas, ones with serious earning potential, but erroneously expect to receive large payment just for sharing it. Unless there's been serious work to patent it, the good idea isn't usually rewarded because the business professional realizes that all the risk and effort are still ahead.

But regardless of how ideas surface, we need good ones. We need a strategy. We must plan our work and then begin to work the plan.

Of course one must consider the known and anticipated obstacles, but these cannot be the overriding focus. If the idea is strong enough, you'll find a way to make it happen. One of the key points in Jerry's books, *The Purpose-Guided Student* and *Why I Teach,* is that "the dream needs to be stronger than the struggle."[1] It's the same way with a business plan—it needs to have worth and possibilities beyond energies expended on obstacles.

While there are numerous guides on developing strategies and plans, few are written for the business community that ties managing to God's teachings. We looked earlier at including God throughout the process as both Senior and Silent Partner. We need to determine the resources and timing in our commitment to proceed. If you don't have time to do it right, then when will you have time to do it over?

Malcolm in the Marketplace

We learn a lot about our management skills when revenues become severely restricted. As I've described earlier, our Ohio facilities went through a tough time of severe retrenchment due to regulatory policy changes. While there were innumerable possibilities before us, in the final analysis there was only one viable option—to reduce expenditures.

We gathered all our facilities' administrators for a luncheon and afternoon planning session; we explored various options and planned our work. We collectively agreed on ways to reduce expenses for a period of time without sacrificing services to our clients. Our managers contributed greatly when they realized what was at stake. This collaboration produced a sound game plan. We weathered a pesky storm and went on to enjoy many more profitable seasons. We planned our work and then worked our plan.

Sometimes the plan can be simple, such as selling the company's jet, reducing overtime, or forgoing the upper end of an advertising blitz. Usually, it's much more complicated, like our time of cutbacks in Ohio. It is always best to seek advice when you are in need of a plan that is much bigger than you. There is not only security in numbers in planning, but commensurate growth in the number of possible ideas generated. "Make plans by seeking advice" (Prov. 20:18).

Using Sacred Space to Find My Business Place

In chapter one we saw that some decisions are routine. Some come without precedent, and others need a thorough response, such as the case with the above crisis in Ohio.

I spent considerable time praying for God's direction during my business days in Ohio. These prayer sessions occasionally occurred at a church campground where I would walk while I prayed. It is a hallowed place, one where God helped me find my life plan and one our denomination consecrated for his work. Like the church sanctuary where my wife and I worship, it was dedicated as a sacred space. Although there may not be anything magical about going to such places, I believe there is something supernatural about being there—being there alone indeed helps me to practice reverence. Like reading a book, it's easy to lose our place in the story. Sacred spaces help us to get back onto the right page, so to speak, and then to read more deeply what's written for us. When schedules didn't permit a trip to the campground, I would skip meals in order to be closer to my Silent Partner—to hear more clearly his voice.

During the Ohio ordeal I struggled to find the thorough response and repeatedly found myself immersed in the Lord's teachings—both in sacred space and making space for sacred lessons. During this time, God revealed his charge in Hebrews 11:6, "Without faith it is impossible to please God." Managing by the Book is much more than using wisdom gained through personal and collective business practices, but doing so in harmony with God's collection of principles and with his guidance.

Big Plans Require Big Planning

Through the years I've been invited to join many big adventures with big plans for big profits. I passed on several of these and they did rather well without my involvement. Life only allows us time to accept a few of these offers. When we are confronted with big plans, or an idea that will require them, we should be struck with the reality that the bigger the plan, the more consuming the planning stage. Or, for those of you in building, the bigger the building you plan, the bigger the plan you build. In essence, both figuratively and literally, the more expansive is the groundwork.

". . . the bigger the bulding you plan, the bigger the plan you build."

When traveling through Europe and Great Britain, I'm always amazed at the scale of the public buildings, many dating to the Middle Ages. St. Paul's Cathedral in London took thirty-five years to build! This project created quite an opportunity for its architect, Sir Christopher Wren. The Great Fire of London (1666) destroyed the original building, which prompted Wren's involvement. He penned a visionary plan and presented it to King Charles II. His sketches pictured a sun-bathed city that would supplant the crowded shambles of Stuart London. He also envisioned magnificent open plazas and wide avenues with the new St. Paul's Cathedral at its center. His plan alone took nine years! Long before CAD programs and architecture software, Wren had to anticipate a myriad of details from load ratios in walls, to water runoff, to the sun's rays refracting through stained glass during the normal times of services. Such a commitment to one plan is nearly unthinkable today in our fast-paced world where immediate results are expected. What he began in 1666 was finished in 1710. It still stands today as a magnificent reminder that a master builder plans his work and works his plan.

Keep Strategic Planning Simple

A top executive of a not-for-profit organization in Florida shared with me that his board was stagnated and did not have a clear picture of how to handle pressing matters. Meeting after meeting ended with no roadmap to lead them into the future. I suggested they have a strategic planning session. I volunteered my services because I had great faith in what they could accomplish with just a little prodding. They were in need of a fresh light to shine on their possibilities, which is a common scenario.

The board agreed to hold a one-day planning session. Upon arrival I discovered they were anxious to take a good hard look at what they were doing and to consider where they should be headed. A strategic plan should answer three very important questions:

1. Who are we?
2. Where are we headed?
3. How will we get there?

Regardless of one's religious commitment, these strategic dynamics are simple and essential.

The board members listed their individual responses to these questions on large flip-sheet poster material. Through this open forum, collective thinking surfaced with the fulfillment of individual contributions.

After a long break, we consolidated their responses and began to forge a unified strategy. The collage became one clear picture. We got there by simplifying their random ideas into five specific tasks. A few years later they realized they had accomplished what had been considered an insurmountable task. There were tangible results from their planning time. The strategy had become manifest in their business reality. The unwieldy chunks were whittled into manageable pieces.

Developing a Team Plan: God as Senior Partner

Stanley Tam, of Lima, Ohio, had a profound influence on my life. He challenged business professionals worldwide with his book, *God Owns My Business*.[2] Tam actually had a lawyer write up a contract between himself and God, making God a majority owner in his business. There were times in his business life that he needed to get an audience with people in higher circles. Since he was the sole owner of his business, he would then call upon God, as his Senior Partner, to gain audience with top executives or politicians he otherwise could not access. Case after case, doors opened.

Stanley Tam kept his promise, and God, as his Senior Partner and majority owner, received fifty-one percent of the profits of the business in the form of donations to religious and charitable organizations. His book encouraged me to bring God more fully into my business—both because of my love for him, and for the benefit of everyone involved (from my family and owners to the employees, and eventually those charities and churches receiving the donations and tithes).

I'm Ending with Your Beginning in Mind

While Christopher Wren's journey may seem distant to your own, there is indeed overlap. If you are early in your career, perhaps still in college, consider your life wedge—that is, what you want to focus on and in which direction you want to head.[3] Now look at the picture of me on the back of this book, or look at any senior business professional—when you join the ranks of the white-haired business veterans, what will be your St. Paul's Cathedral? What will be your main contribution to the business world and, more importantly, how will you systematically use your skills and birthright gifts to further the kingdom? These are questions you need to ask now, and it's my sincere hope that you've glimpsed my heart in this little book. Our success in business may be tied to dollars, but in the face of eternity there are more important dividends worth pursuing.

It is my sincere hope that you have gleaned a point or two from these pages that took nearly forty years of experiences to gather. Most are rather simple, but all are overshadowed by my theology—my belief that God cares deeply about such things.

I have lived out most of my days, but I take comfort in what Catherine Marshall said of her husband, Peter, the renowned Senate chaplain. "It's not one's duration in life that matters, but one's donation." For those of us making careers in business, we might say it's one's donations.

If you're a veteran—perhaps one of my senior colleagues—I'm curious: Are you pleased with how your years have turned out? Is there anything you would like to change?

For most of you, it is not too late to recoup, regroup, and move on without regrets. I have learned that we serve a wonderful Savior. He allows us to have new beginnings if we just ask him. I've certainly made my share of mistakes, and he's been faithful to forgive and to help me to step back into a fulfilling life of serving him through my business.

Each one of us has a bank. Its called "time." Every morning it credits you with 86,400 seconds. Every night it writes off, as lost, whatever of this you have failed to invest in good purposes. It carries no balance, it allows no overdraft. Each day it opens a new account for you. Each night it burns the remains of the day. If you fail to use the day's deposits, the loss is yours.

So, I leave you with these words: spend your time wisely. You cannot go back and retrieve even one second. Thank you for spending your valuable time with me on the pages of this little book. I would like to close with the classic poem by William Allen Dromgoole, the prolific poet from Tennessee (d. 1934).[4]

"The Bridge Builder"

An old man, going a lone highway,
Came at the evening, cold and gray,
To a chasm, vast and deep and wide,
Through which was flowing a sullen tide.
The old man crossed in the twilight dim;
The sullen stream had no fears for him;

But he turned when safe on the other side
And built a bridge to span the tide.
"Old man," said a fellow pilgrim near,
"You are wasting strength with building here;
Your journey will end with the ending day;
You never again must pass this way;
You have crossed the chasm, deep and wide—
Why build you the bridge at the eventide?"
The builder lifted his old gray head:
"Good friend, in the path I have come," he said,
"There followeth after me today
A youth whose feet must pass this way.
This chasm that has been naught to me
To that fair-haired youth may a pitfall be.
He, too, must cross in the twilight dim;
Good friend, I am building the bridge for him."

I trust you are building bridges for those who may be following in your footsteps. May they find it much easier to travel on the highway of life. If we do not leave this world better off than we found it, what is the reason for our existence?

In the twilight of my business and earning years, I'm constantly reminded that monuments that we build for ourselves will, in time, erode away. During the past several years the Lord's teachings have been all the more magnified, along with quips and proverbs that reflect his truths. Each of our lives will soon be past. Only what's done for him will last.

Questions for Reflection

1. In what ways will you apply scriptural principles in your personal and professional strategic planning?

2. If you have not yet developed an accountability group, what will you do in the next two weeks to establish one?

3. How will your relationship with your Senior Partner ensure that you commit all your ways (personal and professional) to him?

4. As you review your current time commitments, what are the four areas that consume the largest part of your week?

5. What steps can you take now to increase the amount of time needed to seek the advice of your Senior Partner?

6. Who will you look to for wisdom when you need to make those difficult decisions in your personal and professional life?

7. What is the most important concept you have learned from this book?

Additional Resources

Bakke, D. *Joy at Work* (Seattle, Wash.: PVG, 2005).

Briner, Bob. *Lambs Among Wolves: How Christians Are Influencing American Culture* (Grand Rapids: Zondervan, 1993).

Maxwell, John C. and J. Dorman. *Becoming a Person of Influence* (Nashville: Thomas Nelson, 1997).

Maxwell, John C. *Leadership 101* (Nashville: Thomas Nelson, 2002).

Reichheld, F. *Ultimate Question: Driving Good Profits and True Growth* (Boston: Harvard Business School Press, 2006).

Sande, Ken. *The Peacemaker: A Biblical Guide to Resolving Personal Conflict* (Grand Rapids: Baker Books, 1997).

Tam, Stanley. *God Owns My Business* (Waco, Tex.: Word Books, 1969).

Appendix

Topical Guide of Advice from the Business World

Harriet Rojas, Ph.D., MBA, MA
Chair of the Business Division
Indiana Wesleyan University

Selected excerpts from Canyon Highlights Perpetual Inspirational Calendar Baylock Originals, Inc. 1999.

- **B**asic
  Instructions
  Before
  Leaving
  Earth

- The best form of spiritual exercise is to touch the floor regularly with your knees.
- Seek the good for all—not just for personal needs.
- Do not pray for task equal to your powers; pray for powers equal to your task.
- Thank God for what you have. Trust God for what you need.
- Reputation is not so much what you stand for—it's what you fall for.
- Behind every face of every person we can see the face of Jesus and hear him say, "I died for this person."
- Purity of soul cannot be lost without your approval.

- It is when you give of your self that you truly give.
- The most important thing in your life is not your position—it's your disposition.
- Prayer is an armor—do not go into your day without it.
- There's only one real way to attain success, and that is to be in the will of God.
- When you walk with God, you will reach your destination.
- God has not called us to see through each other, but to see each other through.
- Live blamelessly; God is near.
- God made you just the way you are so that he can use you the way He has planned.
- Only when we have knelt before God, can we stand before men.
- A lot of kneeling will keep you in good standing with God.
- Love is more than a characteristic of God; it is his character.
- The real measure of your wealth is what you have invested in eternity.
- God never gives up on you!
- Sorrow looks back. Worry looks around. Faith looks up.
- The world is composed of givers and takers. The takers eat better, and the givers sleep better.
- No one knows you as well as God knows you.
- The Christian is not ruined by living in the world, but by the world living in him.
- Live your life so that there will be those that will thank God that you lived.
- Nothing with God is accidental.
- What we are is God's gift to us. What we become is our gift to God.
- Will Christ be revealed through your work today?
- The task ahead of you is never as great as the Power behind you.
- You can't break God's promises by leaning on them.
- Prayer doesn't need proof, it needs practice.

- When you give to God, you discover that God gives to you.
- Christ has no place in your life unless he has first place.
- He who is born of God is certain to resemble his Father.
- If God abides in your home, his presence cannot be hidden.
- God always gives his best to those who leave the choice with him.

Notes

Introduction

1. Business leaders like Stanley Tam have been a great encouragement to thousands of us attempting to balance our business interests with our religious beliefs. Stanley's book about his silver-extraction business in Lima, Ohio, became a standard work in stewardship studies, and his notion of God as Senior Partner became central to my own approach to business. See Stanley Tam and Ken Anderson, *God Owns My Business: They Said It Couldn't Be Done, but Formally and Legally* . . . (Camp Hill, Pa: Christian Publications, 1969; reprinted, Horizon House, 1984). For a condensed version of his testimony, see the text of his speech, "God Owns My Business," (addressed to the annual Generous Giving Conference, Orlando, Florida, February 19–21, 2004), http://www.generousgiving.org/articles/display.asp?id=162.

Chapter 1

1. See the *Dilbert* official homepage at: http://www.dilbert.com/. Scott Adams gives the following profile for "The Boss": "He's every employee's worst nightmare. He wasn't born mean and unscrupulous, he worked hard at it, and succeeded. As for stupidity, well, some things are inborn. His top priorities are the bottom line and looking good in front of his subordinates and superiors (not necessarily in that order). Of absolutely no concern to him is the professional or personal well-being of his employees. The Boss is technologically challenged but he stays current on all the latest business trends, even though he rarely understands them."

2. See: http://www.nbc.com/The_Office.

3. Notes from 1979 lecture on "Strategetics" by Keith Drury, Indiana Wesleyan University, Marion, Indiana.

4. Granville N. Toogood has several helpful little books with creative object lessons for being proactive rather than inactive in our leadership roles. See *The Creative Executive: How Business Leaders Innovate by Stimulating Passion, Intuition, and Creativity* (Adams Media, 2000); *The Articulate Executive: Learn to Look, Act, and Sound Like an Executive* (New York: McGraw-Hill, 1997); *The Articulate Executive: How the Best Leaders Get Things Done* (New York: McGraw-Hill, 1997). Both of the latter two books highlight his POWER formula for making presentations, which also has application in our daily management meetings, e.g., strong start, one theme, good examples to support the theme, ordinary language, and a strong ending.

5. Various resources exist in the business world to assist with this lonely dynamic, e.g., The Young Presidents Organization (for presidents and CEOs under 50); the Young Entrepreneurs' Organization (for those under 40), and TEC Worldwide (formerly The Executive Committee). See Mark Lefko, "It's Lonely at the Top—Who Do You Turn To?" *Los Angeles Business Journal* (August 27, 2001).

6. Richard Swanson, *Margin: Restoring Emotional, Physical, Financial, and Time Reserves to Overloaded Lives* (Colorado Springs: NavPress, 2004), 17.

7. Ibid., 70.

8. See Tom Raft's homepage at: http://www.bucketbook.com/. Tom Raft and Donald O. Clifton, *How Full Is Your Bucket: Positive Strategies for Work and Life* (New York: Gallup Press, 2004); Richard A. Swenson, *Margin: Restoring Emotional, Physical, Financial, and Time Reserves to Overloaded Lives* (Revised, NavPress, 2004).

9. This modern proverb is adapted from Robert Burns' poem "To a Mouse."

10. For a candid appraisal of this topic, see Jason Bayassee, "The Health and Wealth Gospel," *The Christian Century*, July 12, 2005, 20–23.

Chapter 2

1. Matthew Miller, editor, "The Forbes 400," http://www.forbes.com/2007/09/19/richest-americans-forbes-lists-richlist07-cx_mm_0920rich_land.html. "One billion dollars is no longer enough. The price of admission to this, the 25th anniversary edition of the *Forbes 400*, is $1.3 billion, up $300 million from last year. The collective net worth of the nation's mightiest plutocrats rose $290 billion to $1.54 trillion."

2. Jim Collins, *Good to Great: Why Some Companies Make the Leap . . . And Others Don't* (San Francisco: HarperCollins, 2001). See Jim Collins' illustration of Sallie Mae's former CEO, David Maxwell, at: http://www.jimcollins.com/lab/level5/index.html#.

3. Tim Sanders, *Love Is the Killer App: How to Win Business and Influence Friends* (Random House, 2002).

4. In this case we also need to keep in mind that Mohammad (who died in 632), the founder of Islam, plagiarized from other religions including Judaism, Christianity, and Zoroastrianism.

5. Jerry Pattengale, "Heed the Rules or Lose all the Marbles," *Chronicle Tribune,* February 24, 2002.

6. Robert A. Briner, *The Management Methods of Jesus: Ancient Wisdom for Modern Business* (Thomas Nelson, 1995); Indiana Wesleyan University honored Bob's biblically grounded business life with its Society of World Changers. He was the first inductee. This society is based on the thesis of his best-selling book, *Roaring Lambs* (Grand Rapids: Zondervan, 1995); that is, that Christians have done a good job building their subculture, but need to become excellent in fields outside of the church community in order to be salt to a world in need.

7. See Neil Howe and William Strauss, *Millennials Go to College,* (American Association of Collegiate Registrars and Admissions Officers and LifeCourse Associates, 2003); also see David Madland and Amanda Logan, *The Progressive Generation: How Young Adults Think about the Economy,* Center for American Progress, May 2008, http://www.americanprogress.org/issues/2008/05/pdf/progressive_

generation.pdf (accessed May 22, 2008). Also see: "Higher and Higher Education: Trends in Access, Affordability and Debt," Demos, A Network for Ideas and Action, November 28, 2006, http://www.demos.org/pub1160.cfm (accessed May 21, 2008).

8. This section is adapted from Jerry's feature article in "Progress," a special edition of the *Chronicle Tribune* (03/28/04). This article is entitled "The Dawn of the New Business World: Intangible Business Zones."

9. Tim Sanders, *Love Is the Killer App: How to Win Business and Influence Friends* (Random House, 2002), 149.

Chapter 4

1. B. Selcraig, "The Real Robinson Crusoe," *Smithsonian*, July 2005, 82–90.

2. Robert Kraske, *Marooned: The Strange but True Adventures of Alexander Selkirk* (Clarion Books, 2005).

Chapter 5

1. See Jerry Pattengale, "Student Success or Student Non-Dissatisfaction," *Growth Journal,* Spring 2006, 13–25; Frederick Herzberg (1991), *Herzberg on Motivation*. Penton Media Inc. and Herzberg (a summary of his work): "Employee Motivation, the Organizational Environment and Productivity," at http://www.accel-team.com/human_relations/hrels_05_herzberg.html (2005); Jerry Pattengale, Rob Thompson, Kim Parker, "A Purpose-Guided Campus: From Homework to a Mentoring Residence Hall," *Recruitment and Retention in Higher Education* (Magna Publications, January 2008).

2. See F. I. Herzberg, "One more Time: How Do You Motivate Employees?" *Harvard Business Review*, Sep/Oct 87, Vol. 65, Issue 5, 109–120; *The Motivation to Work* (New York: John Wiley and Sons, 1959).

3. See the full text at: http://www.secinfo.com/d1Z3c2.13z.4.htm.

Chapter 6

1. Parker J. Palmer uses the term "birthright gifts." He contends that "Every human being is born with some sort of gift, an inclination or an instinct that can become a full-blown mastery." Some people confuse birthright gifts with techniques and skills that they've acquired through considerable effort. Unfortunately, they build their careers on them instead of using them to complement their birthright gifts. See Palmer, *The Active Life: Wisdom for Work, Creativity, and Caring* (San Francisco: Harper Collins, 1990), 66.

Chapter 7

1. Andrew Carnegie, "Introduction," *The Gospel of Wealth and other Timely Essays* (New York: The Century Co., 1901), pp. xvi–xviii. Carnegie's use of "gospel of wealth" is not to be mistaken for what is often called the "health and wealth gospel" among some suspect sermons. Rather, Carnegie held that "The gospel of wealth but echoes Christ's words. It calls upon the millionaire [billionaire] to sell all that he hath and give it in the highest and best form to the poor by administering it himself for the good of his fellows . . . [before he dies]" (p. 43). See: http://books.google.com/books?vid=OCLC01053245&id=q5ALvRp61w gC&printsec=titlepage#PPR3,M1.

Chapter 8

1. Alden Whitman, "J. Paul Getty Dead at 83; Amassed Billions from Oil," *New York Times*, June 6, 1976.

2. See www.marcprensky.com.

Chapter 9

1. Carnegie, "The Gospel of Wealth," *The Gospel of Wealth*, 19.

2. Ibid., p. 16.

3. Ibid., pp.15–16. Carnegie's advice on modesty among successful business men and women is also worthy of consideration and aligns with

Scripture: "Whatever makes one conspicuous offends the canon [proper standards of behavior in a community] . . . The community will surely judge and its judgments will not often be wrong" (p.16).

4. Dave Dravecky, *When You Can't Come Back* (San Francisco: HarperCollins, 1992), 28.

Chapter 10

1. Jerry Pattengale, *The Purpose-Guided Student: Dream to Succeed* (New York: McGraw Hill, 2010); *Why I Teach: And Why it Matters to My Students* (New York: McGraw Hill, 2009).

2. Carnegie, "God Owns My Business," *The Gospel of Wealth*, 16.

3. See Jerry Pattengale's *Why I Teach* for a fuller description of the Life Wedge Principle (New York: McGraw-Hill, 2008).

4. William Allen Dromgoole was the poet's given name, although she was a woman. She published the majority of her thousands of works under Will Allen Dromgoole, and the first several under Will Allen, and was commonly known as "Miss Will." Her father anticipated a son and gave her the name he had chosen. A special collection of her works is at the University of Tennessee (Knoxville). "The Bridge Builder" appears in numerous settings and in many business discussions. This version is taken from *Masterpieces of Religious Verse,* James Dalton Morrison, editor (New York: Harper & Row, 1948), 342.

About the Author
and Contributors

Malcolm Evans is reasonably well known among many Wesleyan rcles for his business success. A building on the Indiana Wesleyan niversity campus carries his family name. He has served on the boards of diana Wesleyan University, Asbury Theological Seminary, World Gospel fission and the Lakeview Wesleyan Church. He also served key roles in 1e Christian Business Men's Association, and in various missionary rojects through Global Partners. His business experience is wide ranging, from steel manufacturing and transportation to nursing home management. While this text will be his first major publishing venture, he contributed writings on business and stewardship for The Wesleyan Church World Headquarters and the National Holiness Association.

Jerry Pattengale co-developed and managed the late Robert Van Kampen's foundation, and also developed one of the top websites (traffic and ratings) with his Odyssey in Egypt program (1996). He serves on the Advisory Board of Veriana Networks, Inc., the Energize Central Indiana Council, the Governor's Council for Faith-Based and Community Initiatives, the National Board for the Center for Women in Ministry (SWU, S.C.), and recently served on the board for The National Resource Center at the University of South Carolina. In addition to securing considerable funding for various causes, he has also spoken nationally in a wide variety of forums including numerous national broadcasts this year. This business text is one of his six books being published this year. In educational circles he's best known for his text, *Visible Solutions for Invisible Students* (USC) and his theories in W*hy I Teach* and *The Purpose Guided Student*, both new this year with McGraw-Hill Publishers. Jerry is an alumnus of Indiana Wesleyan University where he currently serves as the assistant provost, and has a Ph.D. and MA from Miami (Ohio) and a MA from Wheaton College (Ill.). In 2000, he received the prestigious National Student Advocate Award.

Harriet Rojas has held both financial and educational leadership positions for thirty-two years. She served The Wesleyan Church as a missionary to Peru where she became fluent in Spanish. She was recognized by Lewis-Clark State College as the Administrative/Exempt Employee of the year. She has been active in leadership of Wesleyan Women for eight years, currently serving on the General Executive Committee as financial advisor in addition to being representative for the North Central area and district treasurer for both the Indiana North District Wesleyan Women and the Ladies Retreat Committee. Harriet is an alumnus of Indiana Wesleyan University where she is Chair of the Division of Business. She has a Ph.D. from the University of Idaho, MA from Ball State University and MBA from Capella University.

Dave Dravecky, friend of the author, embodies a story of hope, courage, and perseverance in the midst of dark and overwhelming uncertainty. A Major League baseball star in 1988, his career was ended unexpectedly by recurring cancer in his pitching arm. Dave and his family's story of tragedy and triumph have inspired three books: *Comeback, When You Can't Comeback,* and *The Worth of a Man,* as well as the ministry Dave Dravecky's Outreach of Hope, a nonprofit organization in Colorado Springs, Colorado. The Draveckys realized through their own experiences that one cannot battle cancer alone, and so created this ministry to bring hope for those who hurt. Dave is in great demand as a speaker with a story that reaches all age groups; his messages range from motivational to inspirational to evangelical.